# LETTERS ARE ALWAYS IN MATES!

'Course I had to agree !

Soon, we were talking ten to the dozen and he asked me out ! Can't be bad !

**CHRISTINE DEMPSEY, LONDON.**

## PERFECT TRAVELLING MATES !

Last summer me and my family went up in the train to visit my grandparents, who live in York.

It's a long train journey and we always end up getting pretty bored by the end of it – all except me, that is !

You see, what I do is take a pile of old Mates with me – and long after everyone else has got bored with their books and magazines I'm still giggling away in the corner reading all the readers' letters and things ! Thanks, Mates !

**LOUISE, READING.**

## GIFT-WRAPPED !

I couldn't find my Mates when I got home.

Finally, when I asked Mum, she

said va........ ...... have wrapped the potato peelings in it !"

She had !

Don't know what the neighbours must have thought when I raked through our dustbin to rescue my copy !

It was worth it – even if Mick's face was dirtied by the spuds – but then he always looks like he needs a wash !

**BRENDA JOYCE, WELLING, KENT.**

*Look out for lots of lovely letters like these every week in Mates ! And, remember, we pay good money for every one we print.*

# ALL HERE!

**ARIES (March 21– April 20)**
LIFE: You're a very determined and headstrong girl ! It'll do you good to admit you're wrong sometimes.
LOVE: You're going to meet your match ! Be prepared to be bossed round by that fella next year !
LOLLY: You're too generous with your possessions and money. Don't let that certain someone start living off you !

**TAURUS (April 21–May 20)**
LIFE: The Bull and as stubborn as they come ! It might do you good to give in occassionally to other's advice.
LOVE: Try getting to know him as a good friend, then love can come later.
LOLLY: You think slowly and carefully before spending – sometimes it's nicer to act at once otherwise that bargain will be sold.

**GEMINI (May 21–June 20)**
LIFE: You're really changeable. Trouble is, friends could get fed-up listening to your hysterics. Count to ten before you act !
LOVE: He may like your dual personality but he'll never know where he stands !
LOLLY: What with inflation the piggy bank's feeling it too ! Save just that bit harder 'cos you won't be able to afford that treat next year !

**LIBRA (September 23–October 22)**
LIFE: Your overeating is going to catch up with you ! Start a diet – quick !
LOVE: You're going to meet a fella that, at first ,makes your hackles rise. Be careful 'cos he's the one !
LOLLY: There'll be a reward for that job.

**SCORPIO (October 23– November 21)**
LIFE: You're great to have as a friend, very loyal, but be careful with enemies 'cos you've a need to destroy them !
LOVE: This time you may have to overlook his faults and forgive him – 'cos he won't come back !
LOLLY: You're very careful and save money. Then in a flash you spend it on some thing madly extravagant !

**SAGITTARIUS (November 22– December 20)**
LIFE: You're no good at telling lies ! They can read the truth in your eyes !
LOVE: You've been honest with him, so the ball's now in his court – press him for a decision.
LOLLY: Money holds no importance for you. Start thinking ahead 'cos one day you'll need that pound note

# WHAT D'YOU FANCY GE

## LES IS HEADING FOR THE STARS!

"My personal space ship!" reckons Les. "I've always fancied takin' off an' headin' for the stars!

"Mind you, I s'pose I'd need an extra-large stocking . . . !"

## HAPPY KID!

"I'd like a year's supply of happy dust!" says Terry Baccino of Our Kid. "Then, if I saw anyone looking sad, I'd sprinkle it over 'em – and soon they'd be smiling again!

"I wouldn't need any for myself – I'm always happy!"

## TATTY FINGERS!

"My ideal pressie would be a whole year's supply of black nail polish!" says Freddie Mercury. "There's nothing worse than running out of polish in the middle of a tour!

"I mean, you just can't go onstage with tatty fingers, can you?"

Too right!

## LES WANTS A PUSH-BIKE!

"I used to be dead keen on cycling," says Les of Mud. "Went out every week for a ten mile run!

"Had to give it up when I joined the group, tho'. Now I'd like to take it up again – tho' I can't see me making ten miles now!"

## JUST LIKE STAR TREK!

"What I'd really love is one of those things they have on 'Star Trek'," reckons Anna of Abba. "You know, the transporter that moves people from place to place in an instant!

"It's great having fans all over the world, but sometimes, it'd be nice to do away with all the travelling . . . and get there and back in a second!"

## DONNY HAS 'EM LISTED!

Whenever Donny meets a new girl, he puts her address 'n' phone number in his address book!

"Only trouble is, I've got so many addresses, the book's gettin' too full!" he says.

"So that's what I'd really like for Christmas . . . a brand new book. Then I could start all over again!"

# ING FOR CHRISTMAS?

## ROD'S MAGIC SCREEN!

"I'd like a magic TV screen!" reckons Rod Stewart. "One that showed every single football match that Scotland played in.

"I hate missing them!"

## MIDGE'S MAD ABOUT 'ER!

"I'll settle for Linda Lewis!" says Midge of Slik. "Cor, what a gorgeous bird . . . she's really fantastic!"

"Think Santa'll oblige?"

## AN' WHAT WOULD YOU GIVE THEM?

I'd give Elton a pair of contact lenses!

Well, it'd make a nice change from wearing specs all these years . . . !
Diane Morton, Ipswich

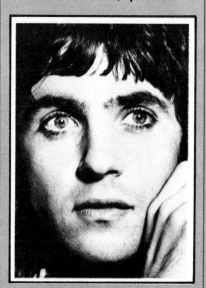

I'd like to give David Essex a punch in the nose!

My bird's been made about 'im for years . . . talks about nothin' else. It's driving me up the wall!
Ronnie Steele, Billingham.

I'd like to give Woody a very special pressie – me!

I'd tie a big bow round my middle, get someone to wrap me up in Christmas paper, and get myself posted – first class, of course!

Imagine if he woke up on Christmas morning and found me there!
Sue Mitchell, Cambridge.

I'd give Noel Edmonds a tea-making machine!

After all, he has to get up really early to waken us up on the breakfast show . . . so I reckon he'd really appreciate a nice cuppa!
Sally Orchard, Hull.

5

# IDEAL GIRL

HEY, SOMETHING SLIPPED OUT OF HIS POCKET..!

AT LEAST THIS'LL BE AN EXCUSE TO CHAT TO HIM AND... HELLO, HE'S BEEN WRITING ON IT..!

WHO IS YOUR IDEAL PARTY GIRL?

Try our Fun Quiz and find out!

1) What is your favourite colour:

    a) red

    b) green ✓

JEEPERS THIS QUIZ HE'S DONE IS A BLUE PRINT OF HIS DREAM GIRL ... SO ALL I'VE GOT TO DO IS FOLLOW THE ANSWERS AND BINGO!

Next morning . . .

WOW, I LIKE YOUR NEW OUTFIT, KATE. WHAT'S THE BIG OCCASION?

NOTHING, I THOUGHT IT'D MAKE A CHANGE, THAT'S ALL. I'VE JUST GOT TO CHECK SOMETHING IN THE LEDGER FILES . . .

8

9

THE END

# THE SADDEST DAY OF MY LIFE!

David Essex can still remember that day . . . the day his world changed from a warm friendly house to one bleak room.

"I was hardly more than a toddler," he says, "but I can remember it quite clearly.

"I'd never been away from home . . . a big block of flats in London's East End.

"It was the friendliest place on earth. Everyone was the best of friends, and we were always laughing. I loved it!"

But then something happened that changed David's life . . . his dad became very ill.

"He'd been ill for a while," he says, "but at first it didn't really affect me very much.

"I was too young to know what was really going on. All it meant was that I'd to be quiet going past Dad's bedroom . . . that I couldn't bring my pals into the house in case we disturbed him.

## BAD NEWS

"Then, one day I was outside playing football with my mates when the doctor's car pulled up and I saw him going into our house.

"He was in a long time, and when he came out again, he looked worried.

"He called me over and told me my mum wanted to speak to me."

David's mum told him his dad had got worse, and he had

to go into hospital.

"It'll make life hard, David," she told him," there's not much money – I don't know if we'll be able to stay on here."

"I didn't really know what it all meant," he says, "except that an ambulance came and took dad away, and after that, mum looked sad 'n' tired all the time.

"Then a few days later, she told me we had to move into a home.

" 'But don't worry,' she said. 'It's just till your dad gets better We'll be home again before you know it – you'll see.'

"We moved out a week later. I'll never forget that day. I had to pack all my favourite toys into a box, and say goodbye to all my pals.

"I was trying to be brave like mum had told me, but I couldn't help feeling scared."

But David didn't cry . . . at least till he and his mum arrived at the home.

## CRIED MYSELF TO SLEEP

"It was the most horrible

place I'd ever seen," he says, "a bleak, forbidding building, with horrible brown paint on the walls.

"And instead of my nice cosy bedroom, I had to sleep in a nasty little cubicle in a big, cold room.

"That night, I just cried myself to sleep. And tho' she tried not to let me see it, mum was upset too."

But in the end David got over his tears and learned to accept his new home.

"Actually, I quite liked it after a while," he grins. "I got used to my little cubicle, and it could be quite fun at times . . . there were always lots of other kids to play with!"

All in all, he was there for nearly a year before his dad was well enough to go home again.

"That was a great day!" he says. "We got a taxi to the hospital to pick dad up . . . that was real luxury!

"Then we all went home . . . home to our very own little flat.

"We were all together again at last – an' I'd never been so happy in all my life!"

# A LETTER TO DANNY

"Cathy — meet Danny," I said, and smiled happily. I'd been longing for them to meet — my new best friend and Danny, the boy I'd loved for what seemed like years already.

It was one of those days that marks the very end of summer; a brown and golden day when the leaves start to fall from the trees to be crunched underfoot. We were outside in my garden, under the big oak tree.

Cath smiled and I could see that she wasn't sure if she was supposed to shake hands with him or not.

He smiled too and their glances met and locked.

Something registered because for a long moment they just stared at each other and I saw Cath's eyes widen and the air became almost electric. It was as if they had forgotten me — I was a million miles away.

It was Danny who broke the spell.

"Hello, Cathy," he said with an embarrassed laugh. "How're you settling in next door and what d'you think of your new town?"

I didn't hear what Cath said because I was thinking of the look that had passed between them. That look had meant something, but what, I didn't know.

It was just a tiny indication of something to come.

### MISTAKEN ?

"Hey, wake up Jill!" Danny was shaking my arm. "I said to Cathy that we'd take her to the town hall dance tonight."

"Course!" I smiled. Surely I must have been mistaken. Danny had his arm flung round my shoulders as usual and Cathy was looking at both of us.

"Lovely!" she said. "What do I wear?"

We discussed all that and Danny sprawled on the grass disinterestedly.

It was really great having a best friend, I decided. Cathy had only moved in next door two weeks ago and already we were really close.

We finally decided what she should wear and what I should wear and Danny lay under the oak tree and laughed at us.

"Whatever you decide on,

CONTINUED ON PAGE 14

# A LOVE STORY TO MAKE YOU CRY...

CONTINUED FROM PAGE 13

I'll be taking the two prettiest girls there," he said.

I looked swiftly at him to see if he was looking at Cathy when he said that, but he wasn't. He almost seemed to be avoiding having to talk to her and look at her directly.

## STRANGE FEELING

"How long have you been going out with Danny?" Cathy asked me when he'd gone.

"About a year, but we've known each other for ages. Childhood sweethearts and all that!"

"That's nice," she said quietly. "I'd like to have that sort of relationship with someone."

"Danny's got lots of friends," I said, "we'll soon fix you up, don't worry."

I was sure Cathy wouldn't have any trouble getting a boyfriend. She was small and pretty, with thick blonde hair that curled onto her shoulders. She had freckles and a little turned-up nose and was altogether exactly the sort of girl that boys usually go for.

That evening she was ready before me and waiting in my house for Danny to collect us for the short walk to the town hall. She only had jeans on, but she had a new top in soft floaty stuff that exactly matched the blue of her eyes and she really did look super.

I was at the top of the stairs when Danny rang the doorbell and she, standing in the hall, opened it.

There was the awful silence again; the strange feeling of being the outsider and that they were the ones in love, in a world of their own.

There was a moment like this and then I heard Danny cough in an embarrassed way.

"Hello, Cathy, don't tell me you're ready on time!" he said. He was trying to sound flippant but I could hear the funny sort of catch in his voice.

I made a big show of coming down the stairs.

"Tar-rar," I said. "How do we look?"

"Great!" he said, again looking everywhere except at Cathy. "Really smashing."

We shouted our goodbyes to mum and dad and Danny offered one arm to Cathy and one to me and we set off.

All the way there I was planning and scheming. I wanted to find a boyfriend for Cathy before this tiny spark of something I'd seen between her and Danny could develop into anything more.

Once there, she had lots of dances. A couple of boys she stayed with for several numbers and I could see her chatting away happily to them.

After every one she came back to Danny and me though, so none of them could have had anything special for her.

As for me, I'd never danced so much. Every time it looked as though Cathy was going to be without a partner I made sure Danny was dancing with me. I don't think at that time that I was really scared of losing him; I didn't think a year of going steady could be wiped out that easily.

But I just didn't fancy taking any chances.

## DANCING CLOSE

Just near the end of the dance, when it got to all the slow numbers, Danny said under his breath to me, "I must have a dance with Cathy."

He got up and held out his hand and Cathy moved into his arms. I watched them carefully, straining my ears with all my might to try and hear what they might say. But they didn't speak at all — not one word — and somehow that was much, much worse.

They seemed to be dancing very close together and sometimes, as they turned away from me, Danny's cheek seemed to brush against her hair, but I may have been mistaken.

They came back and Danny started telling silly jokes, speaking very quickly, and I could see that he was uneasy.

No! I kept saying to myself. No, no. I don't believe it. I'd never been a believer in love at first sight, always thinking that love was something that grew slowly as you got to know each

*I Watched them carefully, straining to hear what they might say. But they didn't speak at all — not one word — and somehow that was much, much worse.*

other, but now . . .

We walked home together. I pulled my jacket around me tightly but the chill wasn't in the evening air, it was from inside me.

"Thanks for taking me — it was a smashing evening," Cathy said at her gate. She didn't even look at Danny as she hurried away indoors.

"I won't come in for coffee tonight," Danny said, "it looks like fog."

"OK." My voice was tight. What could I say? He kissed me and he was a million miles away.

I put my arms around him and kissed him back, trying to show him in that kiss how much I felt, but he was somewhere else . . . I knew he was kissing someone else's lips.

"See you tomorrow?"

"Sure." He waved and was gone.

I suppose I got to sleep eventually that night, but it wasn't easy. I didn't realise just how much Danny meant to me until then, until there was danger of losing him.

Cathy came with us several times after that. It seemed to have become a habit. Every time it was the same — the glances between them, the sudden silences, the feeling that sometimes I wasn't there at all.

I couldn't talk about to it Danny. Any sort of personal, him-and-me talk was impossible these days because he'd always change the subject.

Cathy was acting strangely with me, too. Every time we were on our own she'd keep clear of talking about Danny; if just his name was mentioned she'd get uneasy.

Still I fought against it though. I couldn't, *wouldn't* believe it. Until tonight, that is.

Tonight I knew I couldn't hold on to him any longer.

## CRYING

We were at the club as usual and they danced together—just the one dance like they always had.

As the number finished, though, I saw Danny drop a kiss onto Cathy's head, and as they came back I noticed that their hands were clasped tightly to-gether as if they couldn't bear to be separated.

Cathy sat down in silence but before I got up to have the last dance with Danny I saw one tear slide down her cheek and onto her hand.

I knew then what I had to do. I knew Danny liked me too much — and Cathy did too — ever to hurt me, so I would have to be the strong one.

And now I'm trying to write the hardest letter in the world — to tell Danny that I don't love him any more and that I want to set him free.

Only it's not true. I love him more than I ever did but I must never show that love to the world again.

And, most important of all, I must never let Danny and Cathy know.

They musn't even guess.

Whoever would have thought that that brown and golden day when I brought together the two people I loved most that it would be the one that marked the end for Danny and me?

And now I'm the one who's crying . . . ★

Are your jeans gettin' to the point when they're just about to fall off your bum with sheer exhaustion?!

Well, here's a few ideas on giving 'em a new lease of life!

## SKIRT IT!

For starters cut both legs off to just below the zip.

With some odd bits of material make some gathered frills and sew one to the raw edge of your jeans.

Stitch the next lot onto the hem of the frill before and so on until you've got the length you want. Tart it up with bits of embroidery anglaise or strips of coloured ribbon.

Got yourself a saucy bit of skirt now!

## SHORT'N'SHAPELY

When it starts heatin' up why not chop off the legs of your jeans to bum length and make 'em into cheeky shorts!

You could hem or fray the raw edges.

With the legs make a couple of long strips long enough for braces.

Attach these to the belt loops on your jeans waistband at the back and front with clips.

You're sure to get a few whistles in this little number!

If you don't feel that daring then just cut 'em off to knee length for a great pair of pedal pushers!

## PRETTY 'EM UP!

If your jeans are wearing thin at the knees or seams then smother 'em in embroidery and patches!

Get some coloured beads. Knot one end of the thread and pop on a couple of beads. Now stitch these all the way down the side of your jeans.

If you're good at embroidery then show us how many different stitches you can do by stitching 'em all over the back pockets.

## BAGGED!

Here's another great idea. Chop off the legs of your denims to just below the zip. Stitch straight across on the wrong side.

With the left over legs make 2 shoulder straps and sew to the waistband.

You've got yourself a super strong holdall!

Now you're ready to chuck in your Mates! (The mag we mean!)

## TOP IT OFF!

Fancy a patchwork waistcoat? Well, here's your chance!

Chop your jeans up into 3" squares and sew these all together.

Make one large patchwork piece for the back and 2 smaller ones for the fronts.

Join at the shoulder and side seams.

Get a couple of shoe laces and sew these to the fronts.

Unstitch the back pockets of your jeans and sew one onto each front of your waistcoat.

Pop on your patch waistcoat and you're ready for anything!

## BEADY BELT

Wanna belt round the waist?! All you need are some old denim legs.

Cut 3 long strips and knot one end. Now start plaiting until the belt goes all the way round your waist.

Undo the knotted end and neaten both ends off by overstitching the loose ends until they lie flat.

Get some strands of cord and sew 3 pieces to each end of the belt. Thread on some bright beads and knot the ends of the cord so they don't fall off!

Add some dyed feathers or anything else you've got lyin' around.

Just tie up round your waist!

# WHO'S A JEANIUS, THEN?!

**mates**

FLINTLOCK

**mates**

G. BAND

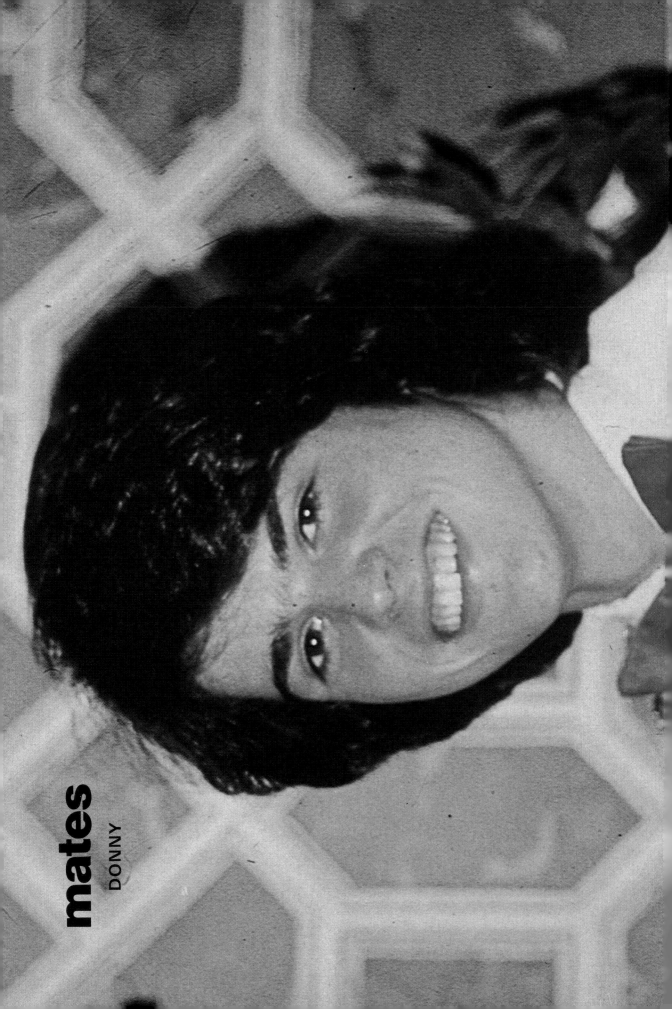

**mates**

DONNY

# NEXT

An apple a day keeps rotten old spots away! Well, it's true, but it takes a little bit more help, too!

## WHAT'S YOUR TYPE?!

For starters you want to sort out your skin type.

Press a tissue first thing in the morning over your face. If it picks up an oily film on the tissue then you're skin probably tends to be greasy.

You'll find the texture of the skin is coarse, especially on the chin, forehead and sides of the nose.

If you only have oily patches across your forehead, chin and nose and dry cheeks then yours is a combination skin.

In the morning if your skin has a tight feel to it and flaky patches start appearing then dry skin is your problem. Rashes and red patches can be the cause of sensitive skins.

## GROTTY'N' GREASY

Right, you've sorted out your skin type, so what's the next step?

Here's how to look after your skin and keep it in great condition.

With greasy skin you might get extra problems, too, like acne and blackheads.

If that's the case then you're not following a regular beauty routine.

Cleansing is the first important step. A clean skin helps get rid of spots and improves the colour.

Wash your skin night and morning with a mild cosmetic soap and in the middle of the day too if it's extra greasy.

Always make sure you remove all your make-up too!

Toning helps to remove the last traces of cleanser and

# OF SKIN!

make-up. Pour a little onto some cotton wool and wipe over your face. Pay attention to the extra oily parts.

Do this night and morning. After toning, your skin will be ready for moisturising. Even oily skins need this to keep it soft and smooth.

Often spotty backs come with a greasy skin so keep 'em scrubbed clean.

A long soak in a bath helps open the pores and really deep cleanse the skin. You could add a couple of drops of TCP to the water.

Check your hair for dandruff 'cos sometimes it falls onto your skin and causes blackheads. Wash out brushes and combs and hair grips regularly.

Get plenty of exercise and fresh air. It's free, y'know, so use up as much as you can!

Careful what you eat, too. Stick to lean meats, fruit'n' veg and lots of milk. Water helps clean you out, so a glass first thing in the morning and last thing at night with the juice of half a lemon added will work wonders for your skin.

If you fancy a nibble have a chew on a carrot or a piece of cheese.

Remember never to touch or squeeze your spots 'cos you'll only spread the germs somewhere else.

You could even cause permanent scarring! Yeuk!!

## WHAT A COMBINATION

With a combination skin you must remember not to use an astringent toner on your dry patches or a moisturiser on the oily bits.

Cleanse with a light milky lotion then tone all over the face with cold water.

For oily parts like nose, chin and forehead use a toner on these. Then moisturise all over and use a richer one for the dry patches.

If you want to use a face mask only apply this to the greasy parts, and try and use a lightly moisturised foundation.

## ALL DRIED UP!

If your skin's a bit on the dry side you should treat it with very rich creams.

First of all you want to cleanse really thoroughly. Choose a milky lotion or cream 'cos these types soften up your skin without drying 'em out.

Next you'll need a toner or you could use very cold water. Wipe gently over your face with cotton wool to remove any last traces of cleanser.

Moisturising is the most important part for dry skins. It helps to protect your skin when you're out of doors. A special tip too is to avoid extreme temperatures.

Never sit in front of a blazing fire 'cos you'll only end up with a flaky shrivelled skin!

Sensitive skins too need a bit of help. You can buy special beauty products especially for people with allergies so watch out for these.

## WHATEVER NEXT?!

Now we've sorted out your skin problems here's a few food tips on how to keep your skin all glowin'n'healthy lookin'!

You'll need a well balanced diet if you want to keep your looks.

For starters make sure you get lots of protein in your diet. It'll help give you shiny hair and a clean skin. Foods like liver, meat, fish and eggs all contain this.

Fats give you energy so things like cheese, bacon, eggs and milk should help you out there.

Vitamins are really important 'cos they help to keep you in fightin' fit condition!

You'll get these from dark green vegetables, fish and fruit. Steer clear of fried foods and try and get your Mum to boil and grill as much of your food as she can.

All fruit is good for you but watch out for bananas 'cos they're the most fattening.

## PACK IT IN!

Face packs are a great pick-me-up for a tired out skin, even if it's dry or greasy. Try some of these.

Grate an apple up and spread it all over your face, leave it for about 10 minutes then wash off.

Cucumbers are a good astringent and great for coolin' down the skin. Simply slice the cucumber up thinly and put them over your face. Leave for about 15 minutes before rinsing off.

Egg whites are just the thing for toning up an oily skin. Spread the raw egg white over your face and leave for a few minutes and wait for it to set. Now rinse off with warm water.

By now you should be ready to face any fella!

# GO ON, BE A SPORT!

Well, are you? The kinda girl who'd do anything (well, almost!) to please? Or are you more likely to smack 'em in the jaw and tell 'em to go and find some other sucker to play with? Try our quiz and find out . . .

**1** You've just managed to scrape together enough money to buy that precious Rollers album, when along comes your best mate with this sob story about how she'll just die if you don't lend her a quid. Do you:–

a. Wipe a tear from your eye and hand over the money – she needs it more than you do.
b. Say, "Get lost, pally, but tell me where to send the wreath!"
c. Tell her that, oh dear, you need all your money to buy a present for your mum. (She doesn't know your mum's birthday was three months ago)?

**2** You and your mate are having a cosy game of strip poker with these two fellas from the youth club, but somehow you keep losing and it's getting kinda chilly. Do you:–

a. Suddenly develop a headache and rush off while you've still got enough clothes on to make a decent exit.
b. Carry on gamely and try to ignore the goosebumps on your bum. Maybe in your next hand you'll get a couple of aces for a change!
c. Refuse to play any more unless the fellas enter into the spirit of the thing and take their knickers off, too?

**3** Big brother, who's lolling in front of the box one wet Saturday watching Match of the Day, asks you if you'd mind nipping down to the off-licence to get him a couple of cans of beer. Do you:–

a. Say, "Only if you give me 50p for going and stop saying that Woody looks like a chimpanzee with his teeth out for the next six months."
b. Empty his packet of salted peanuts over his head and tell him to get up off his lazy bum and go himself!
c. Pull on your wellies and plastic mac and not care if you get half-drowned on the way?

**4** You're out with your new fella when suddenly you bump into Gloria, an old mate of yours who's suddenly gone all blonde and glamorous and looks like she's just had a silicone job (and we're not talking about her nose!). "Please introduce me," says your fella. Do you:–

a. Oblige and resign yourself to the fact that that's the last you'll probably see of him.
b. Say, "Okay, but I warn you, she suffers something awful from bad breath!"
c. Grab him in a half-nelson and say, "Not on your life, pally. Gloria doesn't go in for weeds like you!"?

**5** You know your mate's been up to no good when she rings up to ask you to say she was at your place last night when her mum phones. Do you:–

a. Oblige, adding a few bits and pieces about playing Scrabble till half past ten so her mum's really taken in. You're a good friend, see!
b. Wait till her mum phones and say, "Haven't set eyes on her for a month, not since she met that Fred Fella with the Kawasaki motorbike. Lord knows what they get up to!"
c. Say you'll do it – on condition she'll do the same for you one day!?

**6** Down at the disco there's this bunch of fellas who're mucking about and end up spilling a can of guaranteed-to-stain raspberry juice down the front of your new white dress. Do you:–

a. Pick up a brand new can of guaranteed-to-stain and empty the lot right down the front of his M and S shirt.
b. Accept his apologies and say you'll be sending him the dry cleaner's bill in due course?
c. Bite your lower lip and say that's okay, it was only an accident after all?

## SCORE

1. (a) 0; (b) 10; (c) 5.
2. (a) 5; (b) 0; (c) 10.
3. (a) 5; (b) 10; (c) 0.
4. (a) 0; (b) 5; (c) 10.
5. (a) 0; (b) 10; (c) 5.
6. (a) 10; (b) 5; (c) 0.

### 0–15
*Oh, what a good sport you are! At least you probably think you are, everyone else thinks you're a right walkover! You never say No, never complain, never put your foot down and never lose your temper. You must be looking for a medal or something . . . But you won't get one, you know. Just a lot more errands to run and favours to do. Start thinking about yourself for a change!*

### 20–40
*Congratulations, you manage to be a good sport without being a doormat as well. You don't mind doing favours as long as they're gonna be returned and you'll forgive and forget – as long as it's worth your while. Go on the way you're going and you'll have lots of mates, the kind who respect you. Cos you've got your wits about you, that's for sure, and you let everybody know it!*

### 45–60
*Well, you're no sport, are you? In fact, you seem to go out of your way to score a foul in everything you do. You may be a pretty tough cookie, but one of these days you're gonna meet someone who's just as tough and nasty as you, so you'd better watch out! Either you'd better start mending your ways and try thinking about other people's feelings some of the time – or we'd advise you to go out and do a course in self-defence!*

# GET A MOUTHFUL OF THIS!

# CHEESED OFF!

Here's a really cheapo recipe to give your fella on cold 'n' frosty evenings!

*Now stuff with a slice of cheese and fry up both sides until the cheese starts oozing out!*

*Try and think up some different tasty fillings to fill it up with!*

*One mouthful of that and your fella'll do anything for ya!*

★★★       ★★★★★

*Get yourself a huge thick chunk of bread.*

*Chop off a slice and with a sharp knife make a slit in the slice without cutting the sides.*

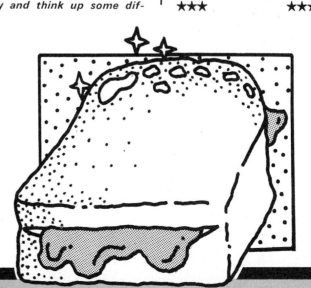

# WHAT TURNS YOU ON?

## TENDER STROKES!

My idea of heaven is to be lying next to a dishy bird on the beach. It's baking hot and she starts rubbing suntan oil into my back.

"Mmmm – the very thought of it makes me feel all warm 'n' cosy. I can't wait for summer to come again!"

## LES LIKES BIG GIRLS!

Give Les a bird with a big chest and it's like handing him a million dollar cheque – honest!

"Whether she's wearing a plunge-line top . . . or got a skin-tight T-shirt. It's all the same to me . . . as long as the proportions are right!" grinned Les.

"It's persuading those lovely ladies to let me get my hands on 'em that's the problem!

"True!"

## WANT A NIBBLE?

I'm a nibblin' guy! No, I'm not that keen on doing the nibbling myself . . . but I love it when a bird chews my ears.

"It's lovely! Mind you, one bird got a bit carried away!

Ended up practically piercing me ear-lobe, she did!

"Nasty that!"

# NOSE AROUND!

If you've got a cute turned-up nose, beware! Real Things's Chris Amoo won't be able to resist tweaking it!

"Sounds mad, I know," confessed Chris. "But little hooters send shivers up my spine.

"They make a girl look so much more kissable, don't they?

"I mean, if her nose sticks up it's so much easier to her lips and give 'em a juicy smacker!"

# ALAN'S BUM-THOUGHTS!

You won't be able to call your bum your own if you waddle past Alan Williams in a tight pencil skirt!

"A tasty-shaped bum is my kinda turn-on," confessed Alan. "I don't care if it's big or small . . . as long as it's a nice shape, and the owner knows how to wiggle it nicely as she walks.

"Yum-yum. Sounds too good to be true!"

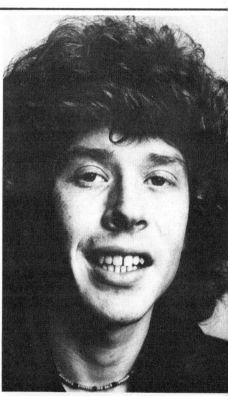

# ROB'S TICKLED!

If a girl tickles me I'm done for!" Rob Davis told us.

"I can't be held responsible for my actions then!"

One of Rob's naughtiest bits is his belly button. One finger laid on his tum and you've got him under your thumb!

# APRÈS SKI..!

FOR STARTERS, I HAD BOTHER GETTING MY FRIEND GLENDA TO COME. SHE'S THE NERVOUS TYPE, YOU KNOW... NOT WHAT YOU'D CALL A SELF-STARTER EXACTLY!

A SKI-ING HOLIDAY? YOU'RE OUT OF YOUR TINY MIND, CAROL — I CAN'T SKI!

WE CAN LEARN, CAN'T WE?

ANOTHER THING... ALAN PERRY AND GORDON JONES ARE GOING. WE'LL BE AT THE SAME HOTEL.

OH! NOW I GET THE MESSAGE...

I'VE BEEN THINKING, IF WE JUST TURN UP ON HOLIDAY, WON'T ALAN AND GORDON THINK — WELL, THAT WE'RE RUNNING AFTER THEM?

STOP TRYING TO PUT OBSTACLES IN THE WAY — I'LL SORT THAT OUT...

"So I booked up for the pair of us — and then mentioned it casually to the boys."

I DON'T EXPECT WE'LL SEE MUCH OF EACH OTHER, CAROL — 'COS I BELONG TO A SKI-CLUB OUT THERE!

YOU'LL SEE LOTS OF ME... I'LL BE LEARNING WITH YOU TWO!

34

THE END

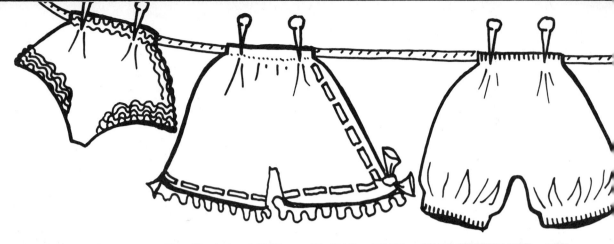

# PICK YOUR KNICKERS FROM THE LINE –AND WE'LL TELL YOU WHAT THEY SHOW!

Pick your knickers

Ever stopped to think how your choice of knickers reveals your personality? 'Cos it does, y'know!

So, next time you bend over, remember that you're revealing more than just your M and S specials, but a few other secrets, too.

Still not convinced? Well, just take a looksee at our line of drawers, pick out the ones that are closest to yours . . . and read on. You're in for a surprise or two!

## CHEAP FRILLS!

This is the giggler! You know, the kind that gets drunk on cocoa and never stops chattering!

They're fun to be with 'cos the fellas are attracted to their bubbly personalities like moths to a flame!

But, they're never serious and break promises easily 'cos they can never remember making 'em!

The frills and lace show that they're also very fussy.

## OOH LA LA!

The tres chic girl! The "butter wouldn't melt in her mouth"

type! This girl usually has a glamorous job and always keeps up with the latest fashion trends.

Trouble is, if she's not careful all her mates will desert her.

Then what's going to

happen if the elastic in her chic knicks goes twang?

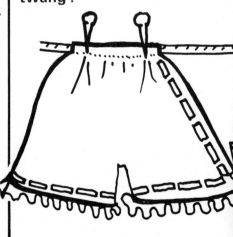

# BLOOMIN' 'ELL!

This is the motherly type of girl. She'd like nothing better than to nab her man, marry and settle down with a family.

She enjoys staying in to watch the telly with her knitting in her lap!

Mind you, she'll have to get out to meet her man first – which could prove a problem 'cos the "cotton bloomer" girl is also basically very shy.

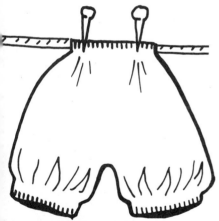

# BARELY THERE!

This girl's life is pretty hectic.

She's fun-loving, very forward and has no wish to settle down – yet!

Usually you'll find her in a crowd surrounded by admiring fellas, but she doesn't have very many female friends. Can't stand the competition, y'see – 'cos, deep down, she's not really as sure of herself as she seems!

# HIP HUGGERS!

This girl's precise and neat and knows exactly what she wants and where she's heading in life – and she always gets there!

But, she'll have to be careful 'cos one day she'll tread on too many toes in her eagerness to succeed.

Like her knickers, the girl's life fits her plans like a glove and she'll come out tops!

# INDECISIVE!

This is the up-and-down girl!

You know, she's really happy and flirtatious one minute; then the next she's in a deep moody depression!

She changes her mind about important issues about as often as she changes her knickers!

It can be frustrating to have her as a friend 'cos you'd never know what to expect from one day to the next!

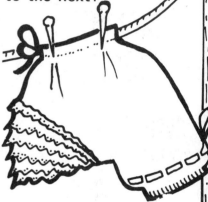

And now that we've revealed all please don't start rushing out and asking all your best mates to bend over so you can have a peek!

If you really want to know what type of knickers they're wearing then just pop round to visit them at home on washing day!

Or arrange to be down the laundrette while their all-revealin' undies are whizzin 'round in the machine!

Simple, yeah, 'cos then you'll know all their secrets – and they won't know you know! ★

# I GOT MIXED UP WITH A ROUGH CROWD!

**At the start it all seemed like a bit of a giggle . . . but pretty soon things began to turn sour!**

It all started when my best mate, Dorothy, started going steady with George.

Before that, we'd always done everything, gone everywhere together, Dorothy and I. But, suddenly, she wasn't interested in me any more. She just wanted to be with George all the time.

Well, you can imagine how I felt. Pretty let down and fed up about the whole thing. For one thing, I didn't have a best mate to go around with any more. And for another, I didn't have a fella either.

Well, you can't really be worse off than that, can you!

For the first two or three weeks I just stayed in at home at the evenings and weekends feeling sorry for myself. I watched so much television I could almost feel my eyes going square . . . and I began to feel like a prize bore as well, with nothing to talk about but what happened on Coronation Street last night or the colour of Angela Rippon's latest twinset.

## AN INVITATION!

So you can't really blame me for accepting when, out of the blue, I got this invitation to a party with a crowd of people I didn't really know.

It was all quite by accident, really. I bumped into this Chris fella outside the supermarket. I'd just been shopping for my mum and was laden down with bags of groceries, when suddenly one of the handles of my carrier bag snapped clean off!

There was this awful crashing, crunching sound as packets and tins scattered everywhere.

Then, to my surprise, this fella all dressed in leather who'd been sitting on a motorbike at the side of the road suddenly got down from it and came across to me.

"Wanna hand?" he asked — then proceeded to help me gather all the bits and pieces up off the pavement.

"I'll give you a lift home if you like," he offered.

"On that, you mean?" I asked, looking at the huge, black motorbike a little apprehensively.

He nodded. "Sure, ain't you never been on one before?"

Well, of course, I hadn't and to tell the truth I felt pretty scared as I climbed up on to the back behind him. But, once we got going, I really enjoyed myself.

There was something fantastically exciting about riding along with the roaring of the engine in your ears and the wind blowing in your face.

When we finally arrived outside my house I was kinda sorry that the ride was over.

## LIVING IT UP!

And that was when he suddenly invited me to come to the party.

"Don't worry," he said, "my mates are a real friendly bunch — and I'll come and pick you up if you like."

That did it.

"Okay,' I said quickly, "but you'd better pick me up at the end of the street. The noise of the bike and everything . . . you know . . . it might waken up my little brother . . .''

"I know what you mean," he said, and winked. "Your folks wouldn't approve if they knew you were taking up with a motorbike gang!"

The words sent a tingle of excitement up the back of my spine. A motorbike gang! Wow, if Dorothy could only see me now — and her snotty little Goerge! — they'd probably just die of shock.

And, as for my parents, of course, well . . . it goes without saying, doesn't it, they would just blow a fuse!

But I didn't care, I was determined to start living it up for a change, to start enjoying myself!

## SHOCK!

Chris had said he'd pick me up at the end of the street about half past eight, and at quarter past I was waiting there, all done up in my best dress and strappy sandals.

It was cold and I felt nervous. What if he changed his mind and didn't

come? I kept asking myself.

But he did come, of course, and I climbed on to the back of his bike like a real expert and we sped off into the night.

The party was right on the other side of our town — a part I'd never been to before — so we had a nice, long ride. I was feeling more excited than I'd ever felt in my life before. This was going to be the night of my life, I kept telling myself. A night I would never forget.

If only I'd known how true that was going to be, I'd probably have asked Chris to turn round there and then and take me home again. But I didn't, of course.

At last, we arrived outside this big tenement block. You could hear the music and laughter from outside in the street.

"Sounds like we've arrived just at the right time," Chris winked. "C'mon, let's go in."

We climbed up some stairs and Chris knocked on the door. A girl with long, blonde hair and lots of make-up let us in . . . and that was when I got the shock of my life!

## THREATENED!

I hadn't expected it to be the kind of party I was used to, but I hadn't expected anything like this, either!

The room was filled with funny-smelling smoke so that you could hardly breathe and there were people draped about the floor, just sort of lying there, smoking cigarettes and passing them round.

I knew straight away what it was. Drugs! They were smoking hash!

And, even worse, there were some couples dancing in the middle of the floor — and they had no clothes on!

For a moment, I just stood there by the door with my mouth wide open, staring in disbelief. I wanted to run, but my feet felt as tho' they were frozen to the ground.

Suddenly Chris turned to me. "What's wrong with you?"

"Nothing," I said, feeling my mouth all dry and sticky as I spoke. "I don't feel well, I want to go home."

"What do you mean? You've just arrived!" Then he gave me a funny look. "You're not thinking of going to the police, are you, Miss Goody-goody? 'Cos you'd better not."

I shook my head. "Of course not. I just don't feel well, that's all."

He grabbed hold of my arm. "I'm telling you, if you try anything like that, you'll be sorry . . . And that's not just a threat, I mean it!"

## ESCAPE!

Suddenly, I felt an awful panic grip

me. Roughly I pulled myself free from his grip and rushed out the door, back down the stairs.

I could hear footsteps thundering behind me, but I just kept running, desperately. All I knew was that I had to escape.

As I ran I could hear him getting closer, and the panic rising inside me was almost suffocating.

What if he caught up with me and dragged me back to that awful place?

What would he do to me? And what would his friends do?

The awful vision of the fate that was in store for me if I once stumbled and fell was burning through my head as I staggered on.

"Oh, please don't let him catch me,.' I kept whispering over and over to myself. "Please, please, anything but that! Please!"

At last I was at the foot of the stairs and I could see the cold light from the lamp-post in the street outside. Breathlessly, I rushed towards it.

## A MIRACLE

Next minute I was out on the street, and the first thing that caught my eye was the big, black motorbike parked at the side of the road.

Just an hour before it had looked so exciting and romantic. Now it seemed to threaten me.

I turned down to the main street. hoping I could catch a bus or something to take me away from there. To tell the truth, though, I wasn't even sure where I was!

Then I heard the noise I was dreading most, the sound of the motorbike engine revving into life.

Oh, Lord, he was coming after me on the bike! It looked as though there was no escape for me now. I could never get to the main road in time — and, even if I did, there'd probably be no-one there to help me.

But then, as I got to the end of the street, suddenly, like a miracle, a taxi appeared and I waved my arms frantically.

Hardly before it had stopped, I climbed inside.

"Take me home," I said to the driver, and as we sped off down the road I suddenly felt safe again and burst into a flood of tears.

I'd managed to escape this time — by the skin of my teeth — and I was so grateful to be alive.

Never again, I promised myself, never again would I take a risk like that. I'd sooner stay in and be bored to death watching television — or maybe, if I was lucky, go to the disco and meet a fella like George.

One thing was for sure — I'd learned my lesson — the hard way! ★

# 8 YEARS AND STILL GOING STRONG!

# THE ROLLE

*Bay City Rollers! Just take a look at this smashing set of pics — and feel free to drool!*

1969

1972

1969: 8 YEARS AGO AND NO PRIZES FOR PICKING OUT THE LONGMUIR BROTHERS!

1972: ALONG CAME ERIC AND THEN THERE WERE 3!

1974: IT'S GUARDS AND AN ARMOURED VAN FOR THE BOYS ON TOUR.

JAN. 1975: SMART IN TARTAN DICKIE BOWS THE BOYS MEET PRINCESS ANNE.

1974

JAN. 1975

1ST. APRIL 1976: HISTORY WAS MADE WHEN IAN REPLACED ALAN.

MAY 1975

OCT. 1975

MAY '75: ESCAPE TO DRY LAND!

OCT '75: FIRST STATESIDE TOUR!

# PS' STORY!

*Memories are made of this! Share them with us now as we relive some special moments in the lives of the one and only Rollers!*

**1973**

**1973:** AS WE KNEW THEM— ON THE THRESHOLD OF BECOMING BRITAIN'S NO.1 BAND.

**MARCH 1975:** REASON TO SMILE! THEY'VE JUST SPENT THREE WEEKS ON A HEALTH FARM AND "BYE BYE BABY" IS ZOOMING UP THE CHARTS!

**MARCH 1975**

**1977:** AND WHAT WILL THE FUTURE HOLD FOR THE BAND WHO'VE GOT EVERYTHING? WHO CAN PREDICT?!

**1977**

# mates

KENNY

**mates**

ROD

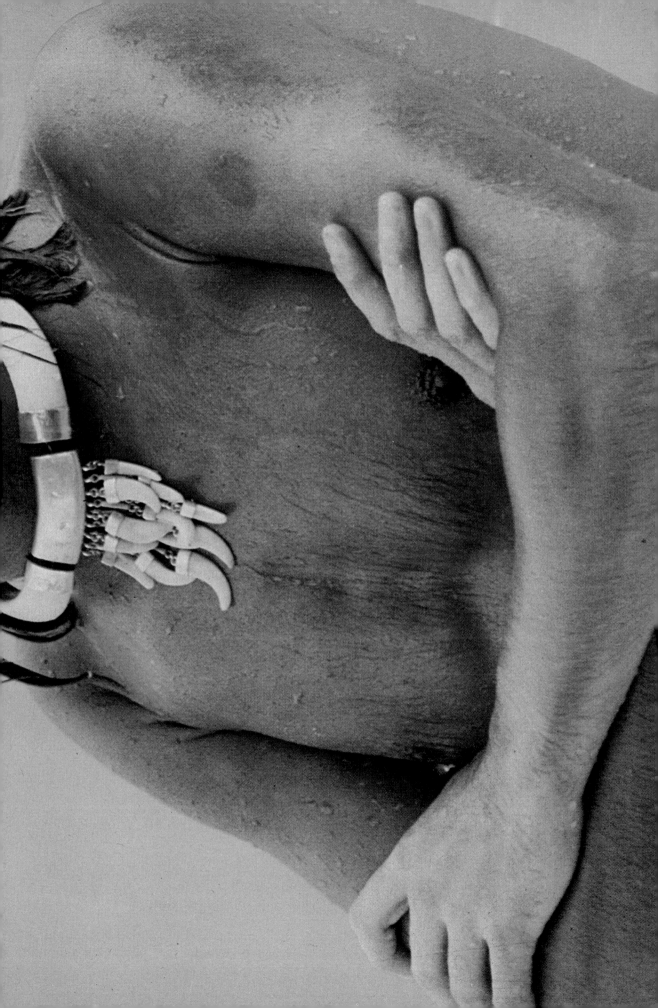

**mates**

ROLLERS

# FANCY FELT FINGS!

Got any scraps of felt lyin' around?
Well it's amazin' what you can do with a needle, thread, and a little help from our mate, Miss Nice'n'Easy!

## PIC-A-POCKET!

Got a dull old blouse that needs a bit of a cheer up?

With a fairly large piece of felt cut out a pocket shape. Now with bright embroidery thread sew a row of stitches across the top.

Next cut out some heart shapes and carefully stitch these on.

Lastly you could end up with your own name or your fella's at the bottom.

All you do is stitch this to the front of your blouse!

## FINGER TIPS!

For some bright ring things cut thin strips of felt just a little bigger than your fingers.

Now stitch the 2 edges together. Make loads and pop on your fingers.

You could decorate each one with flowers, or stitch your name to them.

Make larger ones and use as bracelets. And when they wear out just make some more! Well they don't take that long, eh?!

## PERKY PURSE!

Here's another great idea for carrying around your bus fare!

With 2 bits of felt cut out a couple of squares and round off the bottom corners. Stitch these together leaving the top bit free.

For the flap cut out half a circle in another colour and stitch to the free edge of one piece of the double piece.

Sew a loop onto the flap and a button to match this onto the purse piece.

With a long strip of felt, enough to tie round your waist, stitch to the purse. Easy!

Now you're ready to pop it on round your waist.

It'll be handy for carrying your lipstick in too!

# HOW WE ALL ENDED UP IN THE TOWER...AND NEARLY DIDN'T GET OUT AGAIN!

Don't think we lot ever told you about the day we decided to go to the Tower of London for the afternoon, did we?

Should have known it would end up in trouble – it was Mick's idea, after all.

We'd had a lot of letters from all over the place telling us about the great times you readers had been having.

It was the middle of summer and everyone but us seemed to be on holiday. The office was glistening in the heat and Maggie's pot plants were sending out demands in sign language for more water.

"It's too hot to work," said Mick (not that that's anything to go by cos it's always too *something* for Mick to work).

But this time we all agreed with him – must be the first time ever.

"Why don't we all go out for the afternoon?" he went on.

So that's how we came to be clambering aboard one of those big boats that take tourists for trips down the Thames.

## LEFTOVERS

Gabby was staggering along in front carrying large paper bags full of leftovers she'd begged from the canteen – half-eaten sausages and soggy chips, all that sort of thing, just in case she got peckish.

Mick had generously spent his latest postal order from his granny on cans of ginger beer, Suzi was juggling bottles of moisturiser in insect repellent cos she said the weather conditions would ruin her skin and Carly and Maggie were trying to keep out of everyone else's way so as not to have to carry anything at all.

First calamity happened when Mick opened one of his ginger beer tins. Standing up in the boat like a drunken sailor he ripped the metal disc and next thing we knew a fat lady next to him was hitting him with her tourist guide to London.

## MICK IN A FIZZ!

We soon cottoned on to why she was so mad . . . she was nursing half a pint of loose ginger beer in her lap where Mick's can had fizzed over.

"Stupid boy!" said Gabby.

"Don't you start!" said Mick. Not that we could hear him very well. The fat lady was uttering a string of rude Spanish words at the top of her voice and her husband was showing off his biceps rather near Mick's face.

Gabby started to cheer on the Spanish fella and choked on a canteen sausage.

Suzi jumped up to slap Gabby on the back and fell over a pile of camera equipment belonging to an American gentleman who swore violently and turned out not to be a gentleman after all.

Maggie tried to calm everyone down and ended up shouting at the man in charge of the boat, who pulled in to the shore and made us all get off.

Really, the things that can happen when you try to have a day out with Mick!

We did eventually get to the Tower, though, and we made Mick pay for the entrance fees cos, as we told him, it was his idea in the first place.

We'd have had a nice time in the Tower if Mick hadn't fallen down the stairs and started off the alarm bell so that a whole lot of uniformed officlas rushed in and to him away.

He didn't look very comfortable because his arms were pinioned behind his back and he was pulling the most awful face and squealing.

After that the rest of us thought we might as well go and sit on the grass and eat up what was left of Gabby's food parcels. All that excitement had made us hungry.

## GABBY'S GRUB

Trouble was, some huge blackbirds tried to join in. They dive-bombed us and one of them did a woopsie on Carly's new dress.

Then the Beefeaters came running over and told us we weren't allowed to picnic on the grass.

Carly tried to tell them we were only eating, but they didn't see the difference. Got quite annoyed they did.

That was when we decided it was time to go home.

Didn't see Mick for a week, though. He says they shut him in a dungeon and he kept shouting "Not the block - anything but the block!" Until they let him go on the grounds of insanity.

But we all reckon he slid off to Brighton to visit his auntie for a few days, cos he came back all red and peeling – and you don't get that way in a dungeon.

Whatever happened, it taught us one thing. Never take Mick on an office outing again! ★

Just what does it feel like to be a member of one of the most famous families in showbiz? Well, according to Donny, at times it can be a real drag . . .

You may not believe it, but life isn't exactly a bed of jelly babies for someone like Donny Osmond.

He may look like he's having the time of his life when he's out there on stage, grinning that famous Osmond smile and cracking jokes with the rest of the family . . . but, let's face it, that's what he's paid to do.

And he's got to do it, no matter how rotten'n'glum he may be feeling inside. His folks see to that!

## MY LIFE'S NOT MY OWN!

"Life in a big family like mine isn't always easy," Donny told us. "Apart from the fact that you hardly ever manage to get a moment to yourself, 'cos there's always somebody knockin' on your door or ringing you up at all hours of the day, it's a big responsibility.

In a way, I think you could say that really my life's not my own. Anything I do reflects on my brothers and sisters as well."

Which is why Ma and Pa Osmond keep such a tight rein on their talented little (or should we say big?) brood!

"Can you imagine if I ever got involved in some kind of scandal or something? It would be a disaster — and not just for me, for the whole family!"

Not that we can imagine our Donny ever getting into anything nasty like that.

## THE GIRLS IN MY LIFE!

Mind you, if he ever did do anything a bit naughty, you can bet your last tube of toothpaste that it would be spread across half the newspapers of the world in less time than it takes you to

# IT'S NOT EASY BEING AN OSMOND!

say Utah!

As it is, Donny just has to be seen in the company of a girl more than two times on the trot and everybody's busy speculating if she's gonna be the next Mrs. Osmond!

Which, as far as Donny is concerned, is something that really gets up his nose at times!

"It would be lovely to be left in peace sometimes. I'd love to be able to go out with a girl — or a number of girls — without being followed around by newsmen and photographers all the time.

"And the thing is, I'm usually so busy doing cabaret or touring or recording or whatever that any free time I have for dating is really precious. It makes me mad when some nosy journalists come along and start spying on me!"

## BUSY ALL THE TIME!

It's no exaggeration either when Donny says that most of his life is taken up with work. Even when he's not actually appearing in cabaret or filming for television, there's the endless rehearsing and thinking up stage ideas.

But on the whole, Donny has no complaints. He loves the life he leads — and he's more than a little proud to be a part of a big beautiful family like the Osmonds.

# IT'S THE OLD-TIMERS' PARADE!

Here's Margaret Reid's gran, on the left of the picture. That's her mate on the right . . . seventy years ago!

This is the mate of a gran of a Mates fan (work that one out then!) who lives in Dudley. Quite an outfit, ain't it?

Toni-Lisa Forder sent us this one of her mum, dad, uncles and brothers on a seaside outing. Matey sort of family aren't they?

Couldn't get all the matey mates we'd have liked into the mag – so here's some of the best of 'em.

Shelley Gore's dad and mum got pretty matey while they were young and in love. Shelley says she doesn't think she'll bother falling in love if it means breaking her back at the same time!

Well, you can't get matier than a wedding, can you? So here's Caren Wilton's great-aunt and great-uncle getting wed. Caren's grandmother is the bridesmaid on the left.

Here's Helena Nolon and her sister ten years ago. They're still good mates today – which can be unusual for sisters. Don't they look alike?

# I DON'T CARE IF I DIE!

Dear Maggie,

I met Reg almost a year ago, just after Mum and Dad and I moved to a new town. I didn't know anyone, and since I'm quite shy and not very good at making friends, I was really miserable for a while.

Most evenings I'd just stay in and watch telly or read a book or sit and chat to my mum.

Then Reg came along. (I met him quite by accident – we bumped into each other, literally, in the local supermarket and he asked me out.)

It turned out that he lived quite near me and even went to school close by, so when we started going steady we used to see each other every day. It was fantastic. Suddenly my whole life changed.

Pretty quickly he became the most important thing in my life; I was really in love. And Reg was too.

We used to go everywhere together, do everything together. I think I was happier than ever before.

Then, just a few weeks ago, he suddenly told me he wanted us to finish. Apparently he's met someone else.

Oh, Maggie, I'm absolutely shattered. I don't think I have the strength to go on living without him and, quite honestly, I think it would be better if I was just to die. I know I would be better off.

My life is so empty without Reg. All the time I just want to break down and cry. I just can't cope.

Please help me, you're my only hope.

Well, of course you're miserable. Anyone in your situation would be. You've just lost the fella you love after a year of happiness together, and suddenly you're on your own again.

But it's not the end of the world, you know, and the first thing you've got to do is stop thinking about wanting to die and all that sort of stuff.

If you go on like that you're only going to make yourself even more miserable than you already are.

## DEPENDENT!

It sounds to me as though you became much too dependent on

Reg. Of course, you were new to your town, without any friends of your own, and it was bound to be a temptation to rely on him for company.

But that's where you went wrong!

No-one should ever get to depend too much on another person. (Surely you've heard the old saying about putting all your eggs in one basket?) 'Cos when that other person goes or lets you down, then you're left with nothing – like you are now.

You say that I'm your only hope. Well, I'm glad to be of any help to you that I can.

But your real hope of putting your life to rights lies inside yourself, you know. You've got to learn from the mistake you made and make sure it doesn't happen again.

That means going out and meeting people and starting to make friends of your own. It's not going to be easy, of course,

but it's something you've got to do.

## FORGET HIM!

I know you'll say you can't, but the first thing you have to do is get Reg out of your mind. Stop sitting around and moping. That won't get him back.

And, besides, he's probably out with his new girl friend having a nice time, so why shouldn't you do the same?

He'd probably just think you were being silly if he knew how you were behaving.

And you're not doing yourself any good!

In fact, if you go on the way you're doing you'll end up by doing yourself positive harm. You'll get yourself into such a hopelessly depressed state that you won't be *able* to do anything about it.

So, start pulling yourself together while you can!

You say you're shy and don't make friends easily. Well, believe it or not, lots of us are like that inside. But we make an effort to get out and meet people.

And it's what you've got to do, too!

## FRESH START

In the year you've been in your new town you must have made some friends, even tho' you may not be very close to them. Well, now's the time to start cultivating 'em!

If some girls you know are going to a disco or youth club some night, invite yourself along. You don't have to be pushy, just say casually, "Mind if I come along, too?"

They'll probably be flattered that you want to share their company after keeping yourself to yourself for so long!

And once you're there you'll have the chance to make lots of other new friends as well.

And, even if you don't make masses of friends straight away, at least you're gonna feel a whole lot better just knowing that you're doing something positive about your predicament.

Believe me, it's true.

Once you can manage to shake off that feeling of doom that's shadowing your whole outlook on life right now you'll start to feel a whole lot better about the future.

You'll realise that life is really worth living after all. And it is, you know.

## A NEW LOVE

And another thing, once you start letting yourself live again, chances are you'll meet another fella.

I'm not saying he'll be like Reg or even that you'll like him as much as you liked Reg. But he'll be someone you can share laughs

and secrets with again. Someone who'll make you feel truly alive.

Right now you probably don't believe that. You think there'll never be another fella in your life because no-one could ever take the place of Reg who you loved so much.

But you're wrong – and the day will come when you'll find that out for yourself.

I hope it's soon.

In the meantime, tho', you've got to prove to yourself that you can make it on your own. That life *is* worth living even tho' Reg isn't around any more.

So, please, whatever you do don't just shut yourself away from the world to nurse your broken heart.

We all get our hearts broken from time to time, but hearts mend and life starts again. Believe it, it's true.

Take a tip from me and give it a try.  ★

# WHICH ROLLER'S THE

Ever thought that one day you might end up with one of the Rollers as your fella?
Here's some tips on making it come true!

## CUDDLE UP WITH DEREK!

*If you're the type of girl who likes to snuggle up to a log fire and toast buns all night, then you're definitely the one for Derek!*

*Fashionwise go for soft furry-feelin' jumpers like angora or mohair. So when he snuggles up you'll feel like a lump of cottonwool!*

*Don't go overboard on colours, keep to soft pale pastel shades, you'll look a lot sweeter!*

*When it comes to make-up try and keep it as natural as you can.*

*Go for a beige foundation and smooth on finely.*

*Choose a creamy rust blusher for your cheeks.*

*For eyes nothing fancy here, just a slick of eyeshadow in a pretty blue and then a couple of coats of mascara.*

*Try a clear lip glosser for a more kissable look.*

*Keep your hair in tip-top condition and make it nice and smooth with lots of conditioner.*

## ERIC LIKES 'EM DREAMY!

Are you a bit of a daydreamer, and always making up poems 'n' things?

Well you'd get on like a house on fire with Eric!

If you really want to catch his eye go for a really soft romantic look.

Keep make-up to a minimum and don't overdo it in any way.

Colours should be dreamy and soft, so use some shimmery eye shadow that way he won't be able to take his eyes off you!

If you hair's long why not roll the ends up for a slight curl? Don't forget to use a conditioner on the ends or else they'll dry up and split.

## RAVE ON WITH LES!

Are you a right raver?! Then *Les'll* be after you like a shot!

If you want to make an impression on him try wearing sexy pencil skirts with side slits.

Well, when he gets a flash of leg who knows what might happen!

Tart yourself up with loads of sparkly accessories. But if you really want to capture his heart, don't go without ya tartan scarf!

For ya face don't forget no one's gonna go for a spotty one so keep ya skin nice 'n' clear by cleansing night and morning.

Keep your hair clean too by washing it twice a week.

Go for a curly style and clip the sides back with some combs.

You'll have to wear a comfy pair of shoes when you go out with Les, 'cos you'll be boppin away in some disco till the early hours of the morning if you're lucky!

# ROLLER FOR YOU?

When it comes to clothes go for floaty dreamy dresses and lacy blouses. Ya know, the one's like your granny used to wear!

You want to be sweet smellin' too so dab some scent behind your ears and on your wrists.

One whiff of that and you'll have him under your thumb all evening!

## GET UP AND GO!

*If you're the get up and go type and full of beans then you and Ian could be really great chums! He's the outdoors sporty type. So don't forget your wellies!*

*Make sure you can stand all the windy weather and be armed with loads of moisturiser.*

*Slap it on your face to prevent your skin drying up and flaking off!*

*Keep your hair tucked under a scarf so it doesn't blow all over the place.*

*For make-up you really don't need all that much.*

*Just stick some lip glosser, or Vaseline if you're broke, over your lips.*

*Keep eyes looking clear and natural with a touch of highlighter on the browbone and a light brown shadow on the lid.*

*When it comes to clothes just put your blue jeans on and top it*

*with a cosy stripey woolly jumper.*

*What Roller could resist you now?*

## SOFTLY DOES IT!

Soft and romantic, that's what Woody's girl will have to be like.

No harsh colours but subtle shades to get him in the mood.

Ever thought of going curly? For an irresistible hairstyle roll it up in tiny rollers all over and when it's dry take them out and now run your fingers through it.

It should fall over your shoulders in loads of super natural curls.

Look out for pretty dresses in flowery prints and team up with matching tights.

Just the job!

*By now you should have a good idea on how each Roller likes his girl to look!*

*So choose your look and start searching for that Roller!*

# SUZI PUTS HER FOOT IN IT...AGAIN!

**Y**ou think it's all great fun being a beauty editor, don't you? Go on – admit it!

Well, it is up to a point. I mean, people are always sending you stuff in the post to try out for them. New eye shadows and face packs and nail varnish and all that sort of thing. So that when I've found a nice new look I can tell you all about it.

Mick's always rooting through my post to see if anyone's sent me something good for covering up spots!

Then there are the press receptions I go to, when people who make beauty products ask along all beauty writers for a meal and a demonstration to try out a new make-up.

You can ask any questions you like about what's on show and you learn an awful lot as well as having a great time.

But the other week I went to one which turned out to be a real nightmare!

## HANDS OFF!

The invitation looked alright when it arrived in the post. There it was, all nicely printed on gold paper.

"What's this?" said Gabby, who's always envying my chance to get a good nosh. "Mooshipoo Foot Products? Who are they?"

You may well ask. Actually, Mooshipoo wasn't their real name. But we'll call them that for now.

"Keep your mitts off, Gabs," I said, snatching it away from her. "I'm the beauty expert round here and I'm the one who's going!"

Serves me right I suppose . . .

So after work on the right date I got a taxi to the place where Mooshipoo Products were holding their do.

There was a nice man in gold tights and tabard to show me into the place. Well, I suppose he was a man, I didn't actually ask . . .

When I got inside there were three girls in bunny costumes handing round a tray of drinks. There were loads of other people there, but the bunnies came straight over to me.

"Welcome to Mooshipoo!" they shrieked. "Do you love your feet?"

What do you say to that? I muttered Oh yes, or something, and they gave me a glass of orange juice.

Then it was all rather boring for a while. I didn't know anyone there and everyone else seemed to know everyone except me. So I walked around the room and looked at all the Mooshipoo posters.

They all showed pictures of girls waving their feet in the air and said things like "Mooshipoo makes you walk on air."

The food was all displayed on a table at the back of the room but I didn't like

# MY FEET ARE KILLING ME!

to go and start noshing straight away. So I just stood and stared at it for about five minutes, until I saw some other girl march up, grab a plate, and dig in.

After that there was no stopping me! I will say that for Mooshipoo, they knew how to lay on a good spread.

There were vast plates of sandwiches on gold doillies, a whole salmon cut into slices and decorated with cucumber and olives . . . and even a white and gold swan which turned out to be chicken slices moulded together and covered with a white sauce to make it look like the real thing.

Then there were cherry tarts and huge pineapples stuffed to overflowing with all kinds of fruit.

I made a real pig of myself – and all the other beauty editors started coming up to me to know which dish I liked best – whether the chicken was tough or if the prawns in the vol-au-vents were fresh or frozen.

Got to know quite a lot of 'em that way!

## DISHY FELLA

Then this gorgeous fella came up to me. Really beautiful, he was. Not the sort you find yourself sitting next to on the tube or at the launderette. Long blond eyelashes and a really dishy smile.

"Can I get you another drink?" he asked.

I let him, of course. Hoped he'd get me something stronger than orange juice this time.

When he came back with a glass of wine I beamed and muttered something about could we sit down, my feet hurt.

"Have trouble with your feet, do you?" he murmured, as he guided me to a little tucked-away sofa.

"Terrible!" I said. "Got an awful bunion on my big toe and there's something wrong with my heels, they just collapse under me.'

Had to say something like that or he might have wondered why I was snuggling up to him for support. Couldn't tell him it was the sexy aroma of his high-powered aftershave, could I?

"That's marvellous!" he said, ecstatically. Then, just as my eyebrows were going up and I was about to ask him why, he leapt to his feet and dragged me up to a big woman – and I mean a *really* big dragon of a woman – who was standing by the platform at the end of the room surrounded by all sorts of Mooshipoo products.

"Here, Mabel!" he yelled. "This one's got a bunion! And Athlete's Foot by the sound of it! Terrific stuff!"

He gave me a hefty clap on the back and disappeared.

## STINK!

And that's how I came to be taking off my tights in front of two hundred people and having all my little sores and hard skin shown off to all and sundry. By the time Mabel had finished with my feet I wondered how I'd managed to walk in there on them in the first place.

They gave me bottles and jars and creams and lotions which I'm supposed to cover my feet with three times day. Seems I've got everything short of gangrene!

Funny, but I'd always thought I was quite normal as far as my feet went (which is about up to my ankles).

But if I'm not, what about the rest of me?

Worse, every beauty editor I ever knew has been ringing me up to ask if I'm getting better. Except the one I went swimming with last week that is. She rang to ask if I'd mind not going with her this week cos she doesn't want to catch anything.

Even Mick's got to hear about it and he keeps asking if I want to borrow his socks, 'cos he reckons the stink of them keep his feet healthy.

Personally, I reckon there's nothing wrong with my feet. It's my mouth that's all wrong. I just can't keep it shut at the right times! ★

# KEEPING IT IN THE FAMILY!

Ain't it amazing how musical talent runs in families! I mean, it can't be just coincidence that some of our best groups are made up of brothers (and sisters!). And to illustrate what we mean here's just a few examples . . .

## ROLLER DUO

We couldn't write about famous music brothers and not mention Alan and Derek Longmuir now, could we?

Not only 'cos they were the original members of the one and only BCRs but also 'cos they're too gorgeous to be left out. Know what we mean?

## TWIN CHILD

No, you're not seeing double.

Tim and Keith Atack are the eighteen-year-old twins from Child.

Not only are the brothers identical and share a birthdate of April 5, they've also got the same requirement for a girl — that she should have a sense of humour.

those years ago!

Still, it's incredible to think that the Gibb brothers (Barry, Robin and Maurice) have been in the business over ten years! (They were child stars in Australia at the beginning).

And here's hoping they'll still be around for another few years to come.

## SMILE, IT'S THE OSMONDS!

And, last but never the least, here's the most famous family of them all — The Osmonds.

They've been going for a few years now, but we reckon they're gonna be with us for a long time to come.

We're hopin', anyway!

## BEE GEE BROTHERS

Hard to believe the little pic is the same guys as the bigger pic!

Mind you, they didn't shave all

# HOW TO FEEL GREAT IN '78!

So now the year's coming to an end, and you're looking back on what's been happening in your life, and maybe, just maybe, 1977 was a bit of a nothing year for you.

If that's how you feel, then you'll have to make up your mind to make 1978 a really smashing super year.

Make it the year to change your life!

Starting out on a brand new year is a great excuse for making you into a brand new you!

## GET BUSY!

Just sit down and think of all the things you've always thought you wanted to do.

And then make up your mind to do them!

Dreaming's all very well, but you can't sit back and expect things to *happen*. You've got to get up and make them happen.

Okay, so that cruise around the world or that fantastic once-in-a-lifetime trip to America or India might be stretching things a bit on the pocket money you get, but that shouldn't stop you from making long-term preparations so that one day you *will* go.

Get along to the travel agent and spend a couple of hours browsing through the colour brochures of all those exotic places you'd like to visit, and make up your mind to start a whole new life that will make those visits possible.

Right, so you're still at school. What are you going to do for a career?

Are you going to settle for a really drag job to tide you over till you get married? Or are you going to do something really great so you can enjoy your work? After all, it's going to be at least five days a week, and if you're not happy in your work, that leaves you only two days to be happy in!

Buy Careers for Girls by Ruth Miller (Penguin Handbook) £1·50 and find out what kind of job would suit you.

So maybe school's got a bit much lately. Maybe your mates are leaving and going off to earn some money.

But if you stay on and plan your career by taking the right exams that you'll need, you'll probably end up

much better off than them.

Most jobs that need training or qualifications are better paid than ones which don't.

If you work in a shop selling things, or as a junior clerk, you might be able to manage a week or so in Spain, but it's not going to get you to Bermuda or Japan is it?

If you're really short of money, try and get yourself a Saturday job. It can be fun working in a boutique or a hairdresser's or a record shop.

Or maybe you could set yourself up as a freelance and take dogs for walks, mow lawns, clean cars, do dressmaking, or make toys.

And out of the money you earn, put at least a little of it away to save up for a holiday. You could maybe open a deposit account at the Post Office, or at a bank. Or you might even want to save up money in a building society — for that house you're going to buy one day!

Don't put all your money away though. You want some left to spend on a good time!

## BE EXOTIC!

Make 1978 the year to take up a new hobby. Make it something a bit daft or a bit exotic.

Maybe a touch of karate to get you into the spirit for that trip to the Far East you're planning!

Or take up tap dancing, or even ballroom dancing!

If you're shy and can't make friends easily, then evening classes or sports clubs will soon put a stop to that!

And while you're at it, why not change the way you look, too?

If you've had the same hair-style for over a year now, then it's time for a change. If you've always had long hair, take the plunge and go get it cut into a really fantastic style at a good hairdressers.

Make up your mind to start a weekly grooming session at home.

Start caring properly for your skin. Take a long look at your wardrobe and see if you can't make a few changes there too.

Doesn't have to cost you the earth. Carly's always got plenty of great tips on how to dolly up a set of drab clothes, and if you take a look at all the clothes she chooses for you every week in "Mates" you'll see that she picks cheap but great fashion.

If you've always stuck to wearing the same colours or clothes that are nice but "safe", then splash out on something a bit daring or groovy, or both!

Paint you nails bright red, and then maybe you could dye your knickers to match!

Ring up all your mates and organise a party.

If you're used to going down the disco on a Monday night, why not make it a Tuesday, Wednesday or Thursday instead?

Could be there's been a really dishy fella going there every Wednesday and you've been missing out all this time!

## LEARN THE LINGO!

And just to get you really keen on that holiday you're saving like mad for, you'll just have to start teaching yourself to speak the language!

Ask at your local library for a list of evening classes available, or if you can afford it, buy one of those Linguaphone Courses that come with records or tapes that you do at home.

Send off to a penpal organisation we've listed blow and try and get yourself a penfriend in that country to write to, so that you can really get the feel of the place before you go!

It'll encourage you too, when you're tempted to blow all your savings on a new dress!

Cos when you really think about it, a dress might make you feel good for a

few times when you're wearing it, but a holiday of a lifetime lasts forever because you've got all the memories to live off!

If you really can't afford a holiday why not write to Vacation-Work International (address below), and see a country by working there in the summer! They publish a book called Dictionary of Summer jobs Abroad. It's a great idea!

If your own problems are beginning to get you down, you could always try getting yourself involved in other people's!

If there's an old lady down the road with no-one in the world to talk to except her living room wall, why don't you make the effort and go and see if she wants some shopping.

It's always nice to do something like that because by making someone else happy, you go home feeling good yourself!

Or maybe you could contact some kind of organisation that helps people.

There's a list printed below, so why not write to one of them and see if you can do your bit, too?

Maybe you've not been getting on too well at home lately. Mum and Dad just can't seem to realise you're not a little girl anymore. Maybe you get het up every time they have a bit of a nag at you.

Well, maybe you're right, and maybe they're wrong, but if you could just bring yourself to look at things from their way of thinking, it'll make everything a whole lot easier. Just think how great it would be if there was a really happy, friendly atmosphere at home. *You* can help to make it one, so why not start now?

The main thing about 1978 is that it's going to be *Your Year*.

So get standing in front of that mirror NOW, take a long cool look at yourself. Then, when you've stopped dreaming about the New You that's about to emerge, get down to making the dream come true.

Write down every single thing you're going to do in 1978.

You'll have a fantastic year ticking them all off, one by one!

Have a lovely time!

## USEFUL ADDRESSES

*Vacation-Work International, 9 Park End Street, Oxford.*
*International Friendship League, 16 Beaulieu Road, North End, Portsmouth PC2 0DN (For penpals).*
*National Youth Bureau 17–23 Albion Street, Leicester LE1 6GD. (For information about voluntary work in your area).*
*Help The Aged, 8 Denman Street, London W1.*
*The Invalid Children's Aid Association, 126 Buckingham Palace Road, London SW1W 9SB.*

# POP LUCK

**1** Shade in the dotted areas to find a superstar.

**2** Unscramble the letters to find a hit oldie by Steel-eye Span.

**3** Two of these pics of Rod are exactly the same — can you spot them?

60

# 4

If A = 26 and Z = 1 see if you can work out the name of this hit single from 1976.

**17 6 13 20 15 22 9 12 24 16**

---

# FILL IN THE BLANKS!

**CLUES ACROSS**

1. South American dance (5).
4. Female horses (5).
7. Peters and – – – (3).
8. Go up a mountain (5).
9. The timing of a piece of music or a dance (5).
10. Employ (3).
11. Vapourised water (5).
14. Ornaments worn on the fingers or ears (5).
17. Middle colour of a set of traffic lights (5).
20. Opposite of shuts (5).
23. Tree (3).
24. Goes into liquid – like ice when heated (5).
25. – – – – – John, top pop singer (5).
26. You can get one by basking in the sun (3).
27. Records (5).
28. Shuts violently (5).

5. From Rome (5).
6. Ceases moving (5).
12. – – – Jones, oldie pop singer (3).
13. STEVEN – – – a town (3).
15. Mischievous being (3).
16. Spirit; drunk perhaps with orange or tonic (3).
17. Pointed a gun (5).
18. They can be rung! (5).
19. Takes a break (5).
20. Signs (5).
21. Something added (5).
22. They can be snug (5).

**CLUES DOWN :**

1. Foot coverings worn under the shoes (5).
2. Sweet corn (5).
3. Long-playing record (5).
4. Instrument for measuring the supply of something (like gas) (5).

---

# 5

Shade in some white spaces to find in A and B two D.J.'s surnames and in C and D two super groups.

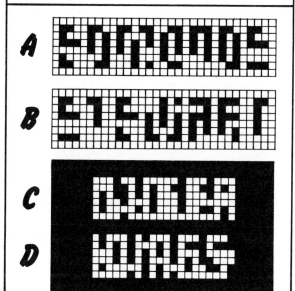

A
B
C
D

## ANSWERS

---

**THE BEST PICS ARE IN MATES!**

# PINTA PUSSIES!

# FANCY A QUICK GRAPPLE WITH FAT FATIMA?

It was a day like any other in the office.

I'd finished my ten o'clock cuppa and was daydreaming 'bout my ideal girl.

There I was, listing my requirements on a piece of paper. She'd have to be about five foot five, slim, with long hair, and just generally someone who'd laugh at all my jokes.

Not too much to ask, is it?

I was getting so involved imagining this girl in my mind that it took some time for me to realise that the office had gone very quiet.

And when things are so silent you know there's trouble brewing.

I was right!

Next thing I knew Gabby came up behind me and started trying to read over my shoulder.

Really annoyed at this invasion of my privacy (nice phrase, eh?; I crumpled my "ideal girl" list and tossed it into the bin.

"Stop being so nosy!" I shouted and stomped off to the canteen for a quick bangers and mash.

## FUNNY PHONE CALLS!

Trouble was, though, that when I came back I got this mysterious phone call.

"Is that Mick, please?"

"Yes."

"I'm Hilary from downstairs."

"It's about your ad in the ladies loo for the perfect girl. I think I fit the description and I'd like to apply!"

It turned out that rotten lot in the office had rescued my bit of paper from the dustbin, added my extension phone number, and stuck it up in the ladies loo!

(I vowed I'd murder 'em when I got off the phone!)

Still, Hilary had a sexy voice and she sounded really nice. She described herself as having blonde hair, five foot six with green eyes.

When she asked me to meet her in the reception after work I couldn't resist.

## ALL TARTED UP!

Hilary said she'd be wearing a dark brown coat and carrying a red bag.

I was feeling quite chuffed as I told Gabby her joke had misfired and how I was just going downstairs to meet this super girl called Hilary.

She didn't say anything, just went a bit red in the face and made a funny choking noise.

Anyway, as the hour of my Big Date arrived I decided to tart myself up a bit. Well, don't want to miss an opportunity like that, eh?

## GINORMOUS!

I walked into our main reception hall, eyes peeled. But there was no sign of the gorgeous blonde I was looking for.

Then I saw this dark brown form and a flash of red!

Hilary! Then as I moved nearer I realised the figure inside the coat was somewhat large – in fact, to be honest it was ginormous!

Suddenly "it" turned round to face me – all smiles!

Blimey! It was that gigantic woman from the kitchens I'd nicknamed "Fat Fatima".

"Oh, Mick," she yelled, everyone turned round to stare, "I've wanted to do this for so long!"

Then she held her arms out wide and enveloped me in about 15 tons of flesh!

I could hardly breathe!

Then she let me go and took hold of my hand, tight.

"I've been looking for someone like you for years!" she said.

(She must have been! She was about forty if she was a day!)

But what could I do? Being a gentlemen, I couldn't just welch on our date, so I took her to the cafe round the corner for a coffee and a jam doughnut (she had three).

Then, while she disappeared into the loo for five minutes I made my escape. Mind you, being a gentleman I paid the bill first!

Still, I daren't go near the canteen these days in case she pounces on me.

So I'm bringing in sandwiches for lunch. Oh well, I suppose it's one way of losing weight!

Funny thing happened in the office one day . . . and now nobody is speaking to me.

It's like this, you see . . . I've got this friend, George. Known him since I was a mere child.

George did everything his mother asked of him. Never threw his apple cores into other people's gardens, always kept his shoes polished – all that sort of thing.

And went into a good steady job in the Civil Service when he was old enough to master Silly Walks (or whatever he needed in his department).

And Mick!

Dunno where he got his gear – he must have borrowed it. A three piece suit! New socks! Even put cover-up stuff on his spots!

Needless to say, tension rose as the morning went on. We were all dreaming about the long, expensive lunch George was bound to treat us to.

Quarter to one came and with it came George.

But a very different sort of George . . .

Filthy jeans with holes in the bum, flip-flops and grubby feet, hair like a haystack.

Only the voice was the same.

# HOW WAS I TO KNOW HE'D FREAK OUT LIKE THAT?!

Funnily enough, I've never minded that George was so different from me. Who else would have always had enough cash put by to take me out, hold my handbag for me in full view of the street when I popped into the ladies loo, or convince my parents that I'd not be grabbed by the forces of the night if I was out after eleven?

(Good one that! It meant I could argue with Mum that if I could be out with George late, I could be out with anyone else late too!)

## DRIFTED APART!

Well, our paths drifted apart, not surprisingly, so I didn't see George for a couple of years after I left school.

So I was very surprised when he rang me up at the office one morning and said that he was back in London after a spell for the Government overseas and could he call in and see me?

'Course, I'd told Suzi and Carly and Mick and Maggie about George. Working with this lot, you can't have any

secrets. Even about extinct fellas.

So by the end of the phone call I'd persuaded him that we were all dying to see him.

And when I put the phone down there was Carly, planning what she'd wear to meet him, and Suzi chipping in too, and Mick muttering about how he'd show that toffee-nosed fella that he wasn't the only one who knew how to dress.

Y'see, we don't have much to do with males of the smooth type around here.

Mick even went out and bought some new socks that afternoon, so you can guess how seriously he was taking it!

## EVENING IN PARIS

Next day, you wouldn't have believed our office. There was Maggie, dusting all the desks and picking Mick's old chewing gum off the telephones, Carly wearing her new cleavage number and Suzi smelling as if it was an evening in Paris rather than a morning in King's Reach.

"How lovely to see you all," he drawled. "I think it's really super of you to club together to take me out to lunch. I've booked a table at that delightful little restaurant by Tower Bridge. They do such perfect oysters . . ."

## FREAKED OUT

They did, actually . . . but George was the only one who ate any. The rest of us were hurriedly inventing strict diets to match our skinny purses.

When we'd got rid of him and were on our way back to the office, they let me have it.

"How was I to know he'd freaked out of the Foreign Office?" I said. "He didn't say so when he rang. Anyway, he's been great to me in the past, spending money like water."

"And it's your own fault for leaping at the chance to meet him!"

So that's why they're not speaking to me any more.

And me? In future, I'm letting bygone fellas be bygones! ★

# DISCO DYNAMITE!

**Meet thepeople who make the music you love to dance to – they're the ones who pack you into the discos every week!**

Call it soul, call it funky, call it anything you like – it's the music that sets your toes a-tapping and your bum a-wiggling so you just have to get up on the old dance floor and do your thing!

In the old days, most of it used to come from America. Just think of all the big funky groups, like the Stylistics, the Four Tops and The Supremes . . . They were the ones who started it – and a lot of 'em are still going strong.

But now a lot more British soul music is getting into the charts.

## A REAL FIND!

Just think of people like Linda Lewis and the Real Thing, for example. Linda's been going for a while, cleverly changing her style over the years to suit the times.

But the Real Thing have only been around in their own right as a top group for a couple of years!

Of course, some disco dynamiters seem to go on for ever. Like Barry White – and, of course, the Stylistics. They're always top.

But the nice thing about this kind of music is that it seems to give everyone a chance. You can be black or white, male or female, a single singer or a group. Anyway you've got a chance – as long as your sound's right, that is!

Look at our own little Tina Charles – five feet nothing of bouncing disco energy – or America's lovely Johnny Nash and Natalie Cole, Abba, the chart-topping foursome from Sweden, or the supremely talented Average White Band.

They couldn't be more different in their styles, but they've all got what it takes . . . the kinda music that just gets you to your feet and makes you wanna dance!

Here's hoping they all keep making a lot more records, for a long, long time to come!

Big Daddy, Barry White

Queen of the Discos, Tina Charles

Going on for ever . . . the Stylistics

# JANE WAS OBSESSED BY HER IDOL!

*He was the only thing I thought about . . . but I didn't realise what my obsession was doing to me until too late.*

# LES McKEOWN RULED MY LIFE!

The funny thing is that in the beginning I never used to be a Rollers fan at all. But then, my mate Judy, who's been crazy about them since I can remember, persuaded me to go to a concert with her. And that was when it happened . . .

I remember sitting there, amid all the screaming Rollers fans, wondering slightly what they were on about, and just waiting for the BCRs to come on stage.

In a way, you couldn't help but get caught up a bit in the excitement and, I must admit, I had my eyes glued to the stage.

Then, suddenly, they were on! It was unbelievable. This strange sharp feeling just went shooting through me at the sight of Les.

I don't know what it was. Partly that bouncy way he has of walking and dancing about, the way he smiles, the cheeky expression on his face. He was gorgeous!

## IN A DREAM

When the concert finally came to an end and it was time to go I could hardly bear to drag myself away. It just seemed too cruel that it should all be over so fast.

I walked out into the street in a dream. I just couldn't get the image of Les dancing about the stage out of my head. It was all I could think of.

Outside the theatre there were thousands of fans waiting to catch a glimpse of the lads as they left.

"Let's hang around for a while and see if we can see them," I said to Judy, trying to sound casual.

"Well, that's a surprise coming from you," she said. "I thought you'd be dying to get home."

Little did she know the way my heart was thumping just at the thought of catching another glimpse of my beloved Les!

We waited for what seemed like hours then, suddenly, this big Rover appeared — and I could tell from the screams that the Rollers were inside.

The crowd surged forward, almost blocking the path of the car. There were policemen and bouncers everywhere, trying to push us all back.

But I was determined they weren't going to push me out of the way. I was gonna catch a glimpse of my idol if it was the last thing I did!

Slowly the car came closer. I was being pushed from all sides, but I didn't care.

And then I saw him! He was sitting in the back seat with Eric, Derek and Woody. They were all sort of squashed up together and they looked a bit scared, I thought.

Then, the next instant they were gone. But that final image of Les was burned in my memory. I would never forget it!

## DEDICATION!

The change that came over me after that night was incredible. I could think of nothing but Les.

At school I would sit and daydream about him, and at night I would lie in bed and fantasise all sorts of stories — always with me and Les in the main parts.

I started spending lots of money on my new dream, too. I bought every single magazine that printed even one word about him (including Mates, of course!) and I began to collect pictures and posters, too.

My bedroom wall began to look like a picture gallery dedicated to Les McKeown.

I even made myself a Rollers outfit and got myself a special McKeown tartan scarf that almost never left my neck.

I was dedicated!

Apart from that, I started saving every penny I could for their albums and singles. I had every one they'd ever cut.

And I started finding out when and where their next concerts were going to be. I was determined that wherever they went I would follow.

I did, too. For the next few months I spent all my free time (plus some time I should have been at school!) going around the country to their concerts, hanging about outside the radio and television studios — anywhere I knew they were going to be.

## GOING MAD!

During that time I didn't see so much of Judy any more. I just wasn't interested in going to discos and parties with my mates any more. After all, Les wasn't going to be there, was he? I would much rather stay at home and listen to my Rollers records and dream my dreams.

Then, one day, Judy took me aside and spoke to me in a way that really made me sit up and think.

"I think you're going mad or something," she said. "It's all very well being a Rollers fan and thinking you're in love with Les, but you're beginning to act like you were going round the bend.

"It's become an obsession with you — and I reckon if you don't take stock of yourself soon you're gonna end up like some kinda loony hermit with no friends at all.

"And I'll tell you something else, I don't think Les would think much of anyone who behaved like you, either."

It hurt to hear her say all that, but she was right, of course. I realise that now. I had taken things too far, I had become completely obsessed.

It took me a while to get back to normal again, to actually stop thinking of Les twenty-four hours a day, but I finally did it.

I still love him, of course, but I think that now if I ever actually met him he might quite like me, instead of seeing me as just some loony fan! ★

69

MY FATHER HAS GOT PLENTY OF MONEY, THANK GOODNESS — BUT TELL ME, WHAT DO YOU DO WHEN YOU'RE NOT WITH ME?

OH, I'M JUST A WORKING GIRL!

For Elly, happy days slid by quickly.

And then . . .

ALL OF THESE HORSES ARE YOURS?

OF COURSE! WELL, THEY'RE DAD'S REALLY, BUT I'M THE ONE WHO RIDES 'EM. HE JUST PAYS!

ELLY . . . I LOVE YOU!

MARK . . !

MARRY ME, ELLY — YOU DO LOVE ME, DON'T YOU?

OH, YES — YES, I LOVE YOU, DARLING. I'LL MARRY YOU IF YOU WANT ME . . !

He took her to meet his parents . . .

WE'RE IN LOVE, MOTHER.

YOU WANT TO MARRY THIS — THIS GIRL?

ALL RATHER SUDDEN, MY BOY!

MY DEAR BOY, WE KNOW NOTHING ABOUT HER. WHO IS SHE? WHO ARE HER PARENTS?

I'M NOT MARRYING HER PARENTS, MOTHER — I'M MARRYING ELLY!

WAIT SIX MONTHS — LET'S GET TO KNOW YOUR YOUNG LADY, MARK.

I'VE WAITED LONG ENOUGH. I'VE KNOWN ELLY SINCE MY BIRTHDAY. WE'RE GOING TO GET MARRIED, MOTHER — **WITH** OR **WITHOUT** YOUR PERMISSION!

DON'T BE UPSET, ELLY. IF MY PARENTS WON'T CONSENT, WE'LL **ELOPE** — WOULD YOU DO THAT?

YES, MARK — WHATEVER YOU ASK.

Then . . .

OH! I — I'M SORRY . . .

MARK, PLEASE DON'T — ANDREW'S HERE!

Before Elly left the house...

ELLY, DO YOU LOVE MARK?

WITH ALL MY HEART, ANDREW — I'D DO ANYTHING FOR HIM!

DON'T LOVE HIM TOO MUCH, MY DEAR. MARK'S NOT AS DEPENDABLE AS YOU MAY THINK . . .

I ALWAYS LOOKED UPON YOU AS A FRIEND, TOO, ANDREW. I WON'T LISTEN TO A WORD AGAINST MARK!

HOW COULD YOU SPEAK ABOUT YOUR OWN BROTHER BEHIND HIS BACK? YOU'VE NO RIGHT!

I — I MEANT NO HARM, ELLY. FORGIVE ME.

Ten days later . . .

MY PARENTS REFUSED PERMISSION, DARLING, SO WE'LL LEAVE TONIGHT, WAIT FOR ME ON THE ROAD AT THE END OF THE DRIVE OF MY HOME. I'LL BE THERE AT ELEVEN-O-CLOCK . . .

YOU WON'T NEED LUGGAGE. I'LL BUY YOU NEW CLOTHES. IN **PARIS** — WE'LL HONEYMOON THERE.

OH, MARK . . . I DO LOVE YOU SO MUCH.

That night . . .

HE'LL BE HERE ANY MOMENT . . . HE MUST BE!

But then . . .

ANDREW? I — I WAS EXPECTING MARK!

I — I DON'T KNOW HOW TO SAY THIS, ELLY — BUT MARK WON'T BE COMING.

MY FATHER FOUND OUT WHAT MARK WAS PLANNING — HE'S THREATENED TO CUT MARK OFF WITHOUT A PENNY IF YOU TWO MARRY!

# IT'S NOT SO BAD BEING A GIRL...

It isn't you know! Even tho' there might be a few times when you've looked at your Mum and Dad and thought how nice it would've been if they'd had a boy instead of you!

The trouble is that when you're a girl growing up all kinds of different things start happening to you.

To your body, to your feelings, to everything about you.

And it can get a bit confusing when you've got to cope with so many different things happening at once.

There you are, happily jogging along in your life, enjoying your childhood, when suddenly you realise you're not the same any more.

## YOU FEEL DIFFERENT!

You start to think differently about things. You start feeling that you'd like to be a bit more independent. You don't want to be with your mum and dad all the time.

You start being aware of boys — not as nice people to play Cowboys and Indians with any more, but as ... well ... they seem different, now.

When your body starts to develop, you can get very shy and awkward about it.

Maybe you've got problems with your skin — spots often appear at puberty because your body's undergoing so many different changes.

And if you've got a spot problem, then everything else can feel rotten too.

The best thing to do is make sure you keep your face scrupulously clean and use a medicated soap like Clearasil to wash your face.

Never touch the spots with dirty hands — in fact try not to touch them at all.

And if your spots get really bad don't hesitate to go along to your doctor, because he'll be able to prescribe some kind of medicine to help the spots disappear.

## BRAS AND PERIODS

There are other things to worry about

too, like breasts (or the lack of them!) Don't worry if you're still flat-chested when all your mates are getting bigger all the time.

We're all different.

Lots of girls feel shy about talking to their mums about things like bras and periods, but you shouldn't really, you know. After all, Mum's been through it all herself, so she'll understand.

But if you've got to the stage where you're wrapping yourself up in layers of woollies to hide a bust that needs a bra, then it's time you went out and bought yourself one.

If you're too embarrassed to tell Mum you need one, just go out and buy a bra along with some other things. Then, when you get home, show Mum what you've bought, and make it casual when you show her the bra.

No problem, see?

Same goes for periods. Your Mum will probably have told you all about them. If she hasn't, ask her!

And don't worry if lots of your friends start theirs long before you. It doesn't mean you're in any way abnormal!

Periods will start at any age between 10 and 17, it just depends on how long your hormones decide to take!

You want to have a chat with your mum, or an older friend or sister, about what kind of sanitary protection you're going to use.

The choice is basically between sanitary towels or tampons. Many people prefer tampons (Tampex, Lilletts) because they're less messy to use and dispose of than towels — and they're more comfortable to wear, too.

Some young girls, though, have problems inserting them, and if you find it at all painful, then it's best to stick to towels.

Make sure you change them at least a couple of times a day, and be extra scrupulous about keeping clean when you're having a period. Otherwise you can end up with a nasty, embarrassing odour problem.

## ACHES AND PAINS

Some girls are unlucky enough to get nasty pains or headaches when they're menstruating, and if that's your problem, it's best to get along to the doctor and see what he can do to help you.

The great thing is to keep active when you've got your period. Exercise actually helps.

And try to make sure you have a good, balanced diet of fresh vegetable and fruit and plenty of protein, and

that you get a lot of exercise.

Then period pains shouldn't be a problem.

Some girls get what's called pre-menstrual tension. They might have a few days of being all on edge or depressed, or their stomachs might swell a bit just before their periods start.

Again, you should go along and see your doctor if that's the case, and he'll be able to help.

And talking of doctors. They can be a girl's best friend, you know! There's no need to feel embarrassed or shy or ashamed of *anything* when you go along to your doctor about female things.

Whether your doctor's a man or a woman, they see plenty of girls your age with exactly the same problems, so they're certainly not going to be shocked or embarrassed by any problem you've got.

## FALLING IN LOVE!

While all these things are taking place inside your body, all kinds of strange things can start happening to your

emotions and the way you feel about — just about everything!

You'll probably fall in and out of love at least a dozen times before you're twenty, so don't think you're being fickle every time you go off a fella. It's only natural!

Falling in love with a pop star is normal, too. And if you find yourself getting an infatuation about a woman teacher or a girl, there's usually no need to worry about *that* either.

Most people go through a stage of thinking they're attracted to someone of the same sex, so there's no need for you to start feeling at all guilty abou tit.

There are plenty of problems that come up when you're a girl, but if you know how to cope with them, to treat them as things you just have to accept and get on with, then you can really start *enjoying* being a girl.

Okay, so you think there's enough to cope with, without having to put up with Mum and Dad thinking you're still four years old.

They probably find it kinda hard to appreciate that their little girl has finally grown up!

## SEX — YES OR NO?

Okay, so maybe they nag a bit and get on your nerves. But most parents only worry and nag because they *love* you. Isn't it nicer to have a mum who cares, than a mum who doesn't mind what you get up to?

Meet your mum and dad halfway on everything, and you'll find your life running perfectly smoothly and happily at home.

One of the problems you'll probably come up against at some time, is getting involved with a boy and having to decide whether to go to bed with him or not.

Of course, only you can decide in the end, but before you do, it's best to really examine your feelings.

Are you saying yes because you're scared he'll leave you if you say no? Cos that's no good. If he threatens to pack you in, then you can be sure he'll just take you and leave you anyway!

Are you really mature enough to cope with all the emotional confusions you're going to experience when you put your relationship on a physical basis?

It's not a question of how old you are. It's a question of being able to cope with the possibility of finding you've given everything to a boy only to end up feeling used and unloved.

Could you face it if he just left you afterwards?

Would you be sensible enough to take proper precautions against pregnancy? How easily could you be swayed, knowing you're taking a terrible risk?

And don't be under any illusions. It can only take the first time — and you could find yourself with a baby inside you. A fond cuddle might seem harmless enough, but sometimes you can get carried away.

## BIRTH CONTROL

If you've already made up your mind about it anyway, you've just *got* to be mature about it, and go along to your doctor, your family planning clinic (address from Town Hall or telephone directory) or to the nearest Brook Advisory Centre (Head Office: 233 Tottenham Court Road, London W1P 9AE. Tel: 01-580 2991.) They will advise you on what kind of contraceptive method you should use.

All of them can help, and you mustn't be scared or embarrassed to go.

Apart from the emotional side, and the risks of pregnancy, there is also a legal side. If you are under the age of 16 it is against the law for a boy to have sexual intercourse with you.

Your boyfriend could get into serious trouble and be sent to court if he has sex with you.

And don't listen to so-called "friends" who tell you that "everybody does it nowadays". It's just not true! There are plenty of fellas around who will want to go out with you because they like *you*.

It always sounds a bit corny, I know, but if you can talk to your mum about things, it makes life a lot easier to cope with.

As I've said, she's been through it all before, even though you might think it was all a long time ago! And things haven't changed that much since she was your age. I bet you'd be surprised to hear some of the things she did!

So, it's worth a try, isn't it? I mean, what with all these problems you're having to cope with, you need someone around who can help and tell you that being a girl isn't so bad, after all! ★

Trouble with fellas is they're just great big bundles of pantin'-hot passion – in the beginning, that is. Then, just as you're starting to feel a bit warm 'n' tingly about the toes, they go and cool down!

So, how do you stop this freezin'-out process?

Well, there's lotsa ways – 20 to be exact! And you can rest assured that they've all been tried 'n' tested by us – and they really work!

# 20 WAYS TO WARM HIM UP...WHEN HE'S STARTING TO COOL DOWN!

**1** Grab 'im when he's least expecting it, then give 'im a big, juicy hug and warm smackeroo about the lips! (Oops, wrong way round! Oh, well, suit yourself.)

**2** Invite him round for a roll on your tiger skin/bearskin/threadbare rug. With warm cocoa for afters, of course.

**3** Knit 'im a jumper with your own fair hands (or your mum's if you can persuade her). Just think how he'll love having all that lovingly-knitted wool wrapped round his person.
PS. Watch out for dropped stitches!

**4** Make him a toffee apple – and one for yourself, of course. Then, when you've munched your way through that, give him a sweet peck on the cheek. That should keep you stuck together for a while.

**5** Tell 'im you love 'im. (Only if you do, of course! And if you don't, what are you reading all this rubbish for?)

**6** Suggest a night out at the piccies. Nothing too serious, of course. A spooky pic will give you the excuse to grab 'im during the shivery bits, and a soppy one will make him feel all romantic and dewy-eyed.

**7** *Invite him round to your place for a nosh – cooked by you, of course. (If your cooking's likely to put him on his back for a week, skip this one and go on to number 8!)*

**8** *Invite him round for a nosh – but get your mum to cook it!*

**9** *Tell him he's the best looking thing since Concorde/Les McKeown/baked beans on toast. (Whatever turns you on!)*

*the holly bush. (But watch out for the prickles!)*

**12** *Send yourself a bunch of flowers and tell him it was from an "unknown admirer". That should get him a bit hot under the collar if nothing else!*

**13** *Take him to the fun fair and book six sessions on the tunnel of love. If that doesn't work, trade him in for a year's supply of candy floss.*

**14** *Listen to his grotty Led Zeppelin albums without complaining for once!*

*you reckon we should have him for a pin-up next week!*

**17** *Next time he's feeling down in the dumps, offer to give him a massage. He'll be like putty in your hands, promise! (But just watch where you're pummelling your fists!)*

**18** *Buy him a bottle of aftershave and hand it over to him with a sexy French accent. (If he doesn't shave yet, he can always use it as a deodorant!)*

**10** *Buy 'im a little pressie. Nothing extravagant and preferably something you can share – like a box of chocs. And let him have first pick – as long as he promises not to snaffle the toffee mallow with the crunchy surprise, of course!*

**11** *Take his dog for a walk. If he doesn't have a dog, take him for a walk – destined to end somewhere suitable, like on the park bench behind*

*You can always go home and revive yourself with a quick burst of the Rollers afterwards!*

**15** *Knit 'im a scarf in his team's colours – and a beret to match if you're feeling really keen. Then he can think of you while he's shivering in the terraces.*

**16** *Lend him your copy of Mates to get him in a good mood, then tell him*

**19** *Laugh at all his jokes, even tho' they're corny. He'll be so chuffed he'll positively glow!*

**20** *As a last resort, if all these fail, buy him a hot water bottle, send him off to bed with it – and go out and find yourself another fella. One that's pantin'-hot and rarin' to go!*

*Ever wondered how you'd match up to some of your favourite superstars?*
*Well, here's a chance to find out!*
*Just pick out the guy and check to see if his sign matches yours. Simple, right?*

**CAPRICORN FELLAS (Dec 21–Jan 19)**
Yan Styles, John (Flintlock), Elvis Presley, Rod Stewart.

WITH CAPRICORN GIRLS – The two together could be rather gloomy as you're both prone to bad moods!

WITH AQUARIUS GIRLS – He's a homely man and you're a party girl. Not a good mix!

complain too much. A short romance!

WITH LEO GIRLS – You'll both quarrel and fight too much!

WITH VIRGO GIRLS – You're too staid for his liking!

WITH LIBRA GIRLS – You're very good for each other!

WITH SCORPIO GIRLS – Avoid each other!

WITH SAGITTARIUS GIRLS – Un-

always be quarrelling!

WITH PISCES GIRLS – Learn to give and take if you want this to work.

WITH ARIES GIRLS – There's no room for two Aries in a relationship!

WITH TAURUS GIRLS – You can't push him around – it'd be unwise!

WITH GEMINI GIRLS – He'll want to take over your life, careful!

WITH CANCER GIRLS – Two clashing personalities – sparks'll fly!

WITH LEO GIRLS – Very fiery partnership!

WITH VIRGO GIRLS – Disastrous! To be avoided!

WITH LIBRA GIRLS – He wants to be boss all the time and you can't accept!

WITH SCORPIO GIRLS – You'll never be friends, let alone lovers!

# PICK A STAR-AND SEE IF HE'S THE ONE FOR YOU!

WITH PISCES GIRLS – You'll both have to learn to accept each other's moods!

WITH ARIES GIRLS – You both see each other's faults and won't forgive them – no go!

WITH TAURUS GIRLS – You'll do well if you cope with his moods.

WITH GEMINI GIRLS – His career comes first and you won't accept this.

WITH CANCER GIRLS – Not compatible, your tempers clash!

WITH LEO GIRLS – You're too outward-going for him!

WITH VIRGO GIRLS – Good match, you're both ambitious!

WITH LIBRA GIRLS – Unwise, you're too wild for his liking!

WITH SCORPIO GIRLS – You're too jealous of his work and it won't work!

WITH SAGITTARIUS GIRLS – He's good with money and you're not!

**AQUARIUS FELLAS (Jan 20–Feb 18)**
Mike Holoway, Kenny Hyslop, Mick Robertson, Brian Spence.

WITH CAPRICORN GIRLS – You're too money minded and he's not – no go!

WITH AQUARIUS GIRLS – The same star signs mix in this case, good match!

WITH PISCES GIRLS – You want all the attention and it's just not on!

WITH ARIES GIRLS – Unwise!

WITH TAURUS GIRLS – To be avoided, you're too jealous!

WITH GEMINI GIRLS – Quite a good match!

WITH CANCER GIRLS – You nag and

comfy partnership!

**PISCES FELLAS (Feb 19–Mar 20)**
Woody, Derek Longmuir, Chris Redburn, Jim McGinlay, Ian & John (Bo Flyers)

WITH CAPRICORN GIRLS – You try to organise and it just won't work!

WITH AQUARIUS GIRLS – Difficult 'cos he wants to be centre of attraction all the time!

WITH PISCES GIRLS – You're both too overpowering, definitely unwise.

WITH ARIES GIRLS – Good union!

WITH TAURUS GIRLS – Could work with hard work from both sides.

WITH GEMINI GIRLS – Your dual personalities makes things shaky!

WITH CANCER GIRLS – Solid relationship 'cos you mother and look after him!

WITH LEO GIRLS – You expect too much from him!

WITH VIRGO GIRLS – You both can't share, so it won't work.

WITH LIBRA GIRLS – You can't understand him at all!

WITH SCORPIO GIRLS – You're very jealous but he copes with it!

WITH SAGITTARIUS GIRLS – Unlikely to work!

**ARIES FELLAS (Mar 21–Apr 20)**
Paul Michael Glaser, Pete (Buster), Elton

WITH CAPRICORN GIRLS – He won't give security you want.

WITH AQUARIUS GIRLS – You'll

WITH SAGITTARIUS GIRLS – You like to be dominated and it'll be a great match!

**TAURUS FELLAS (Apr 21–May 20)**
Rick Driscoll, Gary Glitter

WITH CAPRICORN GIRLS – You're both earth signs and it's a happy union!

WITH AQUARIUS GIRLS – The odds are against you being happy!

WITH PISCES GIRLS – He's too stubborn for your good!

WITH ARIES GIRLS – He's too demanding – not an ideal match!

WITH TAURUS GIRLS – This could be either disastrous or marvellous, if you're both prepared to work at it.
work at it.

WITH GEMINI GIRLS – You'll make great friends but don't let it get serious!

WITH CANCER GIRLS – You get on well together – but make sure it doesn't become boring!

WITH LEO GIRLS – His stubbornness is something you can't cope with.

WITH VIRGO GIRLS – Ideal partners – you live for each other.

WITH LIBRA GIRLS – You have the same interests but tend to argue!

WITH SCORPIO GIRLS – You're both stubborn as mules – watch out!

WITH SAGITTARIUS GIRLS – Life will become impossible after a while!

**GEMINI FELLAS (May 21–Jun 20)**
Alan Longmuir, Noddy Holder, Glenn Fisher (Bo Flyers)

WITH CAPRICORN GIRLS – He can be a flirt and you're too jealous!

WITH AQUARIUS GIRLS – You're very good for each other!

WITH PISCES GIRLS – You'll have a marvellous time at first but don't get too serious!

WITH ARIES GIRLS – You're too dull for him.

WITH TAURUS GIRLS – Don't mistake desire for the real thing 'cos this would be bad!

WITH GEMINI GIRLS – An excellent match!

WITH CANCER GIRLS – He's flirtatious and this could mean sore tempers.

WITH LEO GIRLS – You try to possess him and he'll frighten away.

WITH VIRGO GIRLS – You don't listen to him so he'll find another ear.

WITH LIBRA GIRLS – Excellent partners.

WITH SCORPIO GIRLS – You should avoid each other!

WITH SAGITTARIUS GIRLS – You're both fun loving and should have a great time together!

## CANCER FELLAS (Jun 21–Jul 22)
Kevin (Our Kid), Billy McIsaac, Brian May

WITH CAPRICORN GIRLS – Any long term romance would require patience.

WITH AQUARIUS GIRLS – You could cause him great hurt – be careful.

WITH PISCES GIRLS – You have much in common and it's a good match.

WITH ARIES GIRLS – He won't forgive you if you're unfaithful.

WITH TAURUS GIRLS – If you accept each other's faults life will be marvellous!

WITH GEMINI GIRLS – You're both dreamers and it's not too good to get serious.

WITH CANCER GIRLS – If you learn to adapt to each other it'll be an interesting time.

WITH LEO GIRLS – Avoid each other if at all possible!

WITH VIRGO GIRLS – You're both home lovers which is a great start!

WITH LIBRA GIRLS – He's the outdoor type and you prefer comforts.

WITH SCORPIO GIRLS – You're exactly right for each other!

WITH SAGITTARIUS GIRLS – He needs warmth and you're too cool!

## LEO FELLAS (Jul 23–Aug 22)
David Essex, Johnny Nash, Mick Jagger, Roger (Queen)

WITH CAPRICORN GIRLS – A challenging relationship.

WITH AQUARIUS GIRLS – A stormy partnership.

WITH PISCES GIRLS – Avoid each other if possible 'cos you're not suited.

WITH ARIES GIRLS – Try a bit harder and you'll both come out tops!

WITH TAURUS GIRLS – It's just infatuation, so wake up!

WITH GEMINI GIRLS – You're a challenge to each other.

WITH CANCER GIRLS – Open your eyes to both your faults and you might win through.

WITH LEO GIRLS – If you fall in love it'll be very intense.

WITH VIRGO GIRLS – You just don't take to each other, stay clear!

WITH LIBRA GIRLS – There'll be quarrels, but you both love it!

WITH SCORPIO GIRLS – You're poles apart so stay that way!

WITH SAGITTARIUS GIRLS – You're just right for each other!

## VIRGO FELLAS (Aug 23–Sep 22)
Les, Rob and Kevin (Buster)

WITH CAPRICORN GIRLS – Very nice and easy relationship!

WITH AQUARIUS GIRLS – You'd make good friends, but not much else!

WITH PISCES GIRLS – Watch out for friends trying to break you up.

WITH ARIES GIRLS – Let him go, you're not suited!

WITH TAURUS GIRLS – You're very suited to each other so work on it!

WITH GEMINI GIRLS – Things will fizzle out very rapidly.

WITH CANCER GIRLS – You're prone to pick on each other without cause.

WITH LEO GIRLS – It's not advisable to get serious.

WITH VIRGO GIRLS – Definitely not compatible!

WITH LIBRA GIRLS – He'll not be patient with your extravagant ways!

WITH SCORPIO GIRLS – You differ in lots of ways, too risky!

WITH SAGITTARIUS GIRLS – You'll be great mates, but don't go further!

## LIBRA FELLAS (Sep 23–Oct 22)
Eric Faulkner, Chris (Kenny), Andy (Kenny), Derek, Jim and Bill (Flintlock) Cliff Richard, Midge Ure.

WITH CAPRICORN GIRLS – He likes lots of girls and isn't right for you!

WITH AQUARIUS GIRLS – You're in tune mentally with each other!

WITH PISCES GIRLS – It'll be a tense but very good match.

WITH ARIES GIRLS – Not a very stable relationship.

WITH TAURUS GIRLS – He's a flirt, which you can't accept.

WITH GEMINI GIRLS – You're good for each other 'cos you understand each other's needs.

WITH CANCER GIRLS – You won't be able to hold his attention.

WITH LEO GIRLS – He can't cope with your temper!

WITH VIRGO GIRLS – You'll be very unhappy!

WITH LIBRA GIRLS – It's great at first but won't last!

WITH SCORPIO GIRLS – You're not at all suited together.

WITH SAGITTARIUS GIRLS – You'll have fun if nothing else!

## SCORPIO FELLAS (Oct 23–Nov 21)
Les McKeowan, Terry Baccino (Our Kid), Brian (Our Kid), Bob (Bo Flyers)

WITH CAPRICORN GIRLS – He won't forgive you if you stray.

WITH AQUARIUS GIRLS – You're very bad for each other.

WITH PISCES GIRLS – You're made for each other!

WITH ARIES GIRLS – He's loyal but you'll drive him too far!

WITH TAURUS GIRLS – It'll be a relationship fraught with friction.

WITH GEMINI GIRLS – You're not good for each other.

WITH CANCER GIRLS – A very good match!

WITH LEO GIRLS – You'd be advised to stay away from him.

WITH VIRGO GIRLS – You just don't understand him.

WITH LIBRA GIRLS – You'll find each other very dull.

WITH SCORPIO GIRLS – You both want to be boss, no go!

WITH SAGITTARIUS GIRLS – There's no hope that it'll work.

## SAGITTARIUS FELLAS (Nov 22–Dec 20)
Donny Osmond, Jimmy (Bilbo), Gilbert O'Sullivan

WITH CAPRICORN GIRLS – It's a series of ups and downs!

WITH AQUARIUS GIRLS – You're jealous of his wanderings.

WITH PISCES GIRLS – You'll have a wild time, at first, but don't hope for anything lasting.

WITH ARIES GIRLS – You forgive him his faults and it's a great partnership.

WITH TAURUS GIRLS – Just stay friends and be content!

WITH GEMINI GIRLS – You're both freedom lovers.

WITH CANCER GIRLS – Ooh! One of those love-hate affairs!

WITH LEO GIRLS – You're very good for each other!

WITH VIRGO GIRLS – Definitely not on!

WITH LIBRA GIRLS – When the stars clear it'll be murder!

WITH SCORPIO GIRLS – It won't be easy so work hard on it!

WITH SAGITTARIUS GIRLS – Don't play it too cool and you'll succeed.

# POOH! WH

Are your feet more like a lump of Cheddar cheese or do they have a slight touch of Gorgonzola?!

Just 'cos you hide them away in platforms all the year round doesn't mean they never need any attention!

So get 'em out and let 'em see a bit of daylight. Pooooh!

## FIT FEET!

How would you like to lug around ten sackfuls of spuds every day!

Well, that's what your feet have to put up with. It's not surprising they curl up in agony at the end of the day!

So give your feet a treat and have yourself a pedicure!

First of all give your feet a wash in warm soapy water.

Don't soak them for ages or they'll go all wrinkly like a prune and dry up all the natural oils.

Next dry your feet thoroughly with a soft towel. Make sure you dry in between the toes 'cos this is where the skin starts to crack.

Get an orange stick with cotton wool wrapped round it and soak this in a cuticle remover.

Push back the cuticles with this and remove any surplus. Now apply a cuticle cream.

Trim your toe-nails and cut them straight across with nail clippers. Not too short or rounded at the corners (this stops them from growing inwards.)

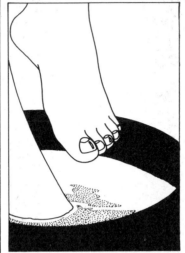

Toe nails grow more slowly than finger nails, so they'll only need a trim once a month.

Finish off the edges with an emery board in downward strokes.

When the skin on the soles gets hard file it off with a special Corn and Callous File you can get from a chemist shop. Or try a Rough Skin Remover cream.

Now with some cream massage this into your feet in upward strokes. Start at the toes working to the knees.

If your feet get sweaty then spray on a foot freshener.

Powder lightly between the toes to get these areas really dry.

Now you're ready to paint on your favourite nail varnish.

Separate your toes with cotton wool and apply the colour carefully.

## EXERCISE WISE!

Putting your feet up relaxes them and gets the circulation going when you're feeling exhausted.

Kick off your platforms and lie back with both feet high up against a wall. Lower them after 2 or 3 minutes and repeat.

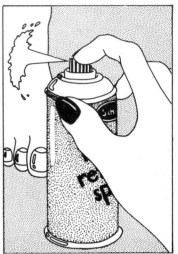

Here's a few more exercises to tone up weak muscles and help strengthen your arches for all you flat footers!

Rise up on your tip-toes slowly and down again. Yep, that's all you do, but it really gets those muscles going!

Another one is to walk on the outer edges of your feet. This is great for toning up your arches.

Try drawing a circle in the air with your big toe. First in one direction then the other. That's a good one for trimming down ankles.

To get your toes in tip-top shape try standing on top of a thick book, like a telephone directory, with your toes hanging over the edge.

Now bend down as far as possible. Do this about ten times.

## WHAT'S THE TROUBLE?!

You won't feel as if you're walking on air if you've got a couple of bunions, more like walking on a bed of nails!

Foot problems can be very painful, but you can stop 'em before they start!

Athlete's Foot can be very nasty! You can catch this

# TA STINK!!

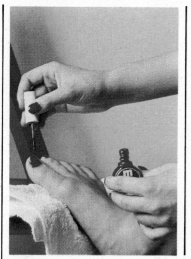

the right size and that your tights aren't too tight. These can all cause cramping and corns !

Your shoes should be half an inch longer than your foot and fit snugly at the heel and instep.

When you next try on a new pair of shoes make sure you stand up and walk up and down in them.

Just 'cos they feel comfy when you're sitting down, they might hurt like anything when you take a couple of steps. Also the sole should be as wide as your foot.

Leather or fabric shoes are

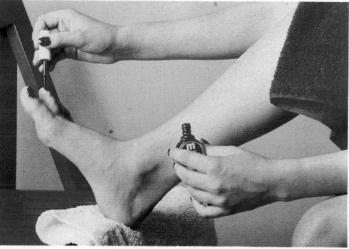

off towels, in showers and swimming pools.

You'll start getting an itchy rash and the skin will start splitting between the toes.

Sounds more like a horror film doesn't it !

You can get some foot powder which will help to clear it up.

Verrucas are another painful thing to have.

These look more like warts and usually are on the sole of the foot. It'll really hurt when you put your weight on it !

A trip to the doctors should sort this one out !

Make sure your shoes are

ideal as they allow the feet to breathe, so no smelly feet !

## TART 'EM UP !

Now you're feet should be worth a second look how about making them more noticeable ? !

Pretty 'em up for those summer days ahead !

Try painting each toe a different colour or paint them a plain colour and sprinkle some silver glitter over them to add a sparkly touch. You can get a small bottle of this

from most stationers.

Or plait some coloured ribbon together and tie neatly round your ankles.

You could also thread up some bright beads on some elastic and wear them on each ankle. Make a couple and wear them at the same time.

A cheaper idea is to wear your bracelets on your ankle. You'll look a stunner on the beach !

When it's winter-time wear a plain pair of tights with some stripey sox for a fun look !

## STICK TO IT !

Right then, now ya know what to do to keep ya tootsies in tip toe condition !

But just to make quite sure here's some rules to go by :
1. Give your feet a pedicure at least once a week.
2. Wash tights after you've worn them.
3. Walk around the house barefoot as often as you can. It'll give 'em some air !
4. Carry a foot spray around with you to avoid nasty smells. You can have a quick squirt and no-one will know !
5. Get shoes soled and heeled regularly.
6. If you have to stand for a long time then tighten up the muscles in your thighs, then relax again. Do this several times. It won't seem as if you're standing around for so long.
7. When you get home put your feet on a stool to get the circulation going !

mates

BUSTER

**mates**
DAVID

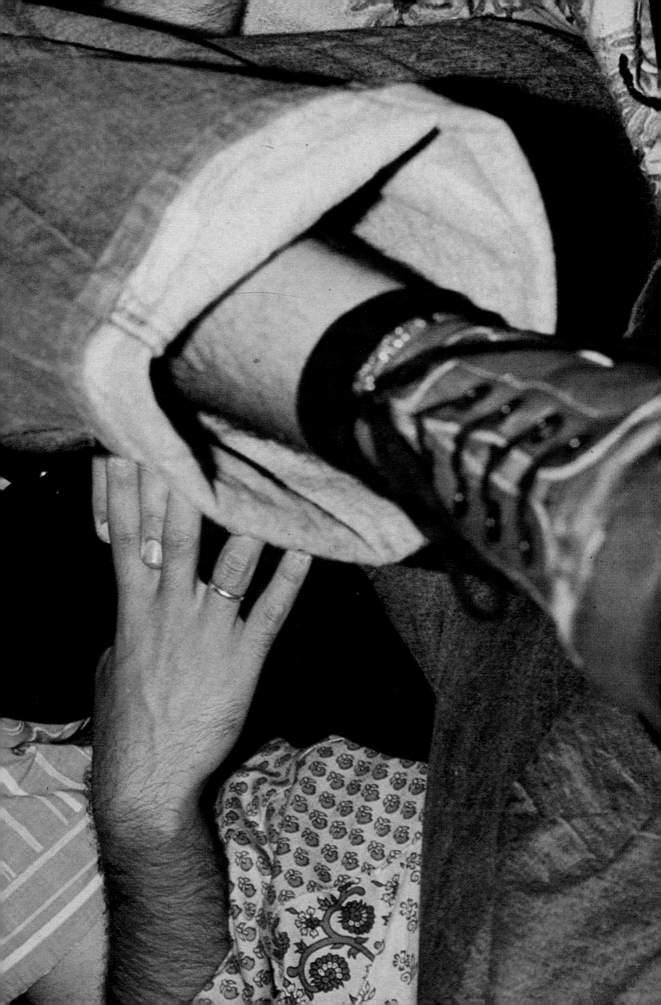

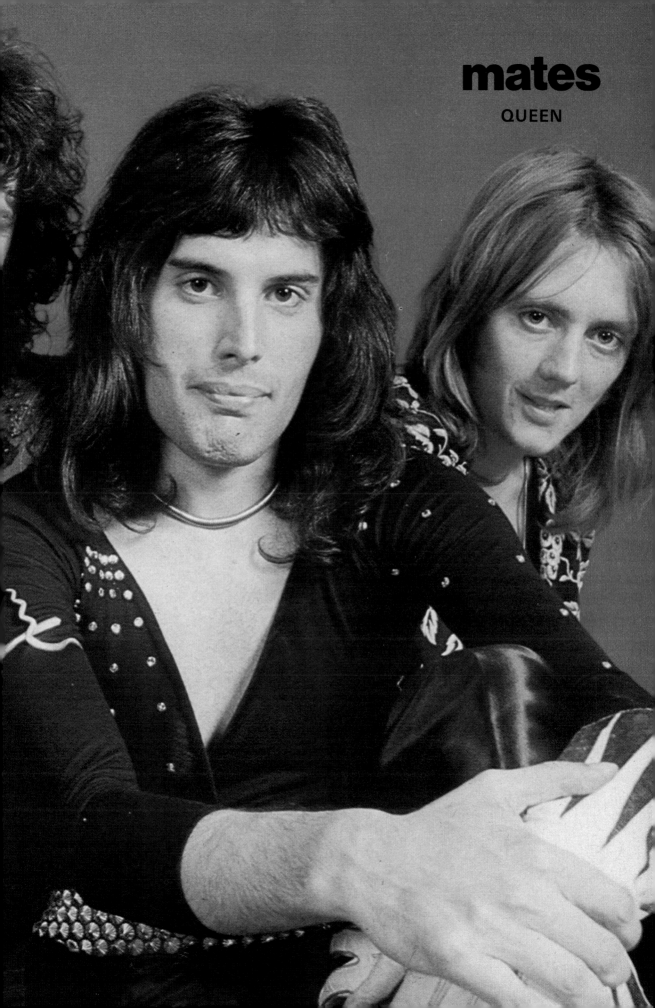

Okay, so right now he's all sweetness and light. Takes you to the back row of the Odeon on a Saturday night and holds you tight during the slow numbers down the disco.

But when it comes to the crunch do you reckon he *really* goes for you? A little or a lot? I mean, if you were flat broke and dying of hunger would he share his last bag of chips with you?

Answer these questions and find out! (And better check some of your answers with him to make sure you're right!)

## HOW TO TELL!

**1.** Does he know when your birthday is – the exact date?
**2.** Has he ever stood you up on a date?
**3.** Does he know what your favourite colour is?
**4.** When you're going out together does he always ask you where you'd like to go?
**5.** If you told him a secret, would you know it was safe with him?
**6.** Does he know what colour your eyes are?
**7.** If you invited him home to meet your folks would he go along gladly?
**8.** If he's gonna be late for a date, does he always ring you up to warn you?
**9.** Do you reckon he'd come to see you even if there was a bus strike on?
**10.** Does he hold hands with you in public?
**11.** When you go out together does he always insist on paying?
**12.** When you quarrel is he always the first to apologise?
**13.** Does he always laugh at your jokes?
**14.** Does he always give you a good night kiss?
**15.** Does he ever ring you up and chat to you for hours – about nothing in particular?

**16.** Would he give up an evening with his mates to be with you?
**16.** Does he often tell you how nice you're looking?
**17.** If you were ill, would he come round with some grapes and a pile of mags to keep you company?
**18.** Does he tell you things he's never told anyone else before?
**19.** Would he go along with you to a Bay City Rollers concert, even though he hated them?
**20.** Has he ever told you that you're the best thing in the whole world?
**21.** Would he buy you a bunch of flowers on your birthday?
**22.** Does he ever buy your copy of *Mates* for you?
**23.** Would he forgive you if you went out with another fella?
**24.** Does he dress to please you?
**25.** Does he always act friendly with your mates?

## NOW ADD IT UP!

Now all you've got to do is add up your score. Award yourself 3 points for every Yes answer; 2 points where you answered Sometimes or Maybe; and 1 point for every No.
Now read on . . .

## WELL, IS IT LOVE?

**57–75**
What a mighty score! This fella of yours would sure do just about anything for you, we reckon, including sharing his last bag of chips! In fact, he'd more than likely give the whole lot to you!
Romeo had nothing on this fella! Looks like he's so besotted with you that you're the most important thing in his life — if not the only important thing!
All that may sound pretty nice and flattering, but do you really want a bloke who puts you up on a pedestal like that and worships the very ground you walk upon? It could begin to be a bit of a bore after a while. He's just too good to be true!

**38–56**
Congratulations! This guy really cares about you, and you can bet your last bottle of vinegar that he'd share his last bag of chips with you!
He's pretty nuts about you, but he's still got his head screwed on all right. He's not likely to let you take over his life and rule him completely — but then you wouldn't want that anyway, would you?
Mind you, we wouldn't put it past him to forget the occasional birthday or maybe even not notice that you've got a new dress on.
But don't let that put you off — a guy like him is worth hanging on to!

**19–37**
He likes you alright, but, let's face it, he's not exactly head over heels, is he? He can be pretty loving when it

suits him (or when he remembers), but it looks like he's got lots of other things on his mind.
That's okay as long as you're not desperately in love with him, but if you are we can only warn you to beware! Get any more involved with this fella and you could end up getting hurt.
Try to play it cool like him!

**1–18**
Who's foolin' who? You must know that this fella's as likely to share his last bag of chips with you as he is to fly to the moon.
Face up to it, sister, he doesn't really give two hoots for you!
Okay, so he maybe finds you fun to be around from time to time, but it would hardly break his heart if you suddenly disappeared in a puff of smoke, would it? In fact, he'd probably not even notice you'd gone!
Unless you're a real glutton for punishment, forget this one and go and find yourself a fella who actually notices you for a change.
There's bound to be plenty around!

# WOULD HE SHARE HIS LAST BAG OF CHIPS WITH YOU?

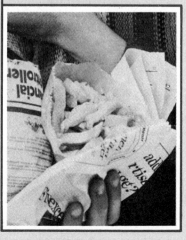

# THE LOVE POTION

I'd always thought Jen's Great-Gran was a bit of a witch . . . but I never guessed her magic spell would actually work!

Jenny found the book with the recipe for a love potion in her Great-Gran's book collection. I'd always thought Jen's Great-Gran was a bit witchy – and this confirmed it!

Some ingredients we couldn't find and we just had to put substitutes in. For instance, I couldn't gather yew leaves at midnight when I had to be in at eleven, could I? I changed that to midday and wasn't even quite sure that it was a yew tree. It might have been an elm – I never was all that good at botany. Then there were herbs and leaves, bark of trees and pollen from flowers. It was a mad idea, but then I was desperate.

"The main thing is the intention," said Jenny seriously. "If you intend it to be a love potion – then it will."

"I wish I could believe you," I said, sighing.

"Well, anything's better than hanging around mooning after him," she said. "At least you're doing something about it."

"I 'spose so – I wish you'd try it out on someone else first though."

"How can I? I don't want anyone falling in love with me. Anyone else, that is," Jenny said, pounding and stirring busily.

It was all right for her, she'd been going steady with Robin for six months and didn't have all the worrying and wondering bit to do.

## MY LAST HOPE

Jenny gave a final stir and I looked at the mixture doubtfully.

"It doesn't look very, er . . . romantic, does it?" I said. "More like stagnant pond water. How am I going to get him to drink it?"

"That part of it," she laughed, "is your problem."

I held the mixture up to the light. "It's full of little bits and pieces."

"We'll have to liquidise it!"

We went into Jenny's kitchen, poured the mess into her mum's liquidiser and switched on. After a minute all the bits and pieces had vanished, leaving a smooth dark green paste. It still looked revoltingly undrinkable though!

"This is ridiculous!" I burst out. "He'll never drink that!"

Jenny gave me a hard look.

"Look, you've tried everything else," she said seriously, "this is your last hope."

I had to agree. I'd been crazy about Ian for weeks and he never took the slightest interest in me. I'd danced right close to him at the disco, passed him messages via his friend Phil and even managed to be standing in his path whenever he walked home, but none that had made the slightest bit of difference. I could have been a cardboard cut-out of a girl for all the interest he took.

"What's wrong with me?" I'd asked Phil last week. 'I'm not that bad, am I?" I could always talk to Phil, he was nice

and kind and understood how I felt about Ian.

"It's nothing to do with how you look," he said. "It's just Ian. He's got exams and football and his mates — he doesn't want to know you at the moment."

It was the next day that Jenny and I found the recipe for the love potion and we started gathering all the stuff to make it. And now, here I was, holding a bottle of foul-looking green sludge and wondering how on earth I could get Ian to drink it. Phil, again! He'd think of something.

## TO THE RESCUE

"You see," I said to him that evening, "I've got this love potion and I want Ian to drink it."

I'll say this for Phil, he didn't burst out laughing or anything, just smiled quite kindly and said resignedly, "And I suppose I'm the one who's got to give it to him?"

"Exactly!" Phil made everything sound so simple.

"Look, let's have a couple of dances and we'll think hard and see if we can come up with anything," he suggested.

We danced together, me casting anxious glances over his shoulder at Ian, who sat surrounded by his mates and completely unaware that a certain someone — me — was eating her heart out for him just a few feet away.

"If it was the olden days," I said to Phil," I'd have one of those rings with a secret compartment then when I passed where he was sitting with his drink I'd just flick the lid open and the potion would fall in."

"Is it a tablet then?" he asked with interest. "That's easy."

"Not exactly," I said. "it's more like green sludge. Come outside and I'll show you."

I got my bag and we went outside and sat on the little patch of grass outside the club. I held up the bottle.

"You've got to be joking!" he said. "You can't expect anyone to drink that!"

"It's all right! It's been liquidised and it's quite clean."

He unscrewed the cap and sniffed. "It smells revolting! He'd realise he had something in his drink a mile off — and it probably tastes like nothing on earth."

## KISS

He put the bottle to his lips and, before I could stop him, took a sip.

"Ugh! It's unbelievably foul! No one could drink it!" he said.

I stared at him. "You just did," I said in a small voice.

He grinned a small, secretive grin. "So I did."

We looked at each other. "That means . . ." I said doubtfully.

"It means that the spell's going to work on me now," he said. "And to make it just right — you should have some too."

He held the bottle to my lips and before I could think about it, I'd swallowed a tiny drop.

"Oh," I said in dismay, "I didn't want . . ."

He put his arms around me. "I could have told you ages ago that Ian wasn't right for you," he said.

"No?"

"No. But I am."

"Really?"

His arms tightened around me and he kissed me and all at once I knew that he was right. I couldn't think why I hadn't realised it before.

I broke away and looked into his eyes.

"Is it the love potion?" I whispered. "Did it work?"

He laughed. "Who knows?" he said.

He kissed me again then and the magic was right there, and whether it was the love potion or not really didn't seem to matter any more! ★

91

# OUR WEEKS WITH THE ROLLERS!

**Angela Matthews is a mad Roller fan, so one day, she made a special trip to Scotland to meet the group – and ended up staying weeks!**

"We live in London," wrote Angela, "but we thought the best way to meet the boys was to go all the way up to Edinburgh.

"We arrived in Scotland on Tuesday, and went straight to Tam Paton's house.

"We'd only been there for a little while when a taxi came, and inside it was Eric!

"Then a couple of minutes later, Ian arrived. We were in heaven, 'cos my mate Tina likes Eric, and I like Ian!

"We waited at Tam's all that day and the next, we saw all the Rollers coming and going."

## HID!

"Then, the day after that, the Rollers all went up to Eric 'n' Woody's farm to do some filming, so we went up there too and watched them filming.

"After that, we saw the Rollers somewhere every day.

Some of the time, Eric was staying in a hotel, and we went past the hotel and saw their Range Rover, so we hid behind it and waited until Woody 'n' Eric came out.

"Then we got their autographs and took their photos.

"They were really nice – much nicer than we'd expected them to be!"

## SCARED!

"Another time, we met Les when he arrived at Edinburgh Airport. His mum and dad were meeting him off the plane, and we stood and talked to them all for nearly an hour!

"But the best day of all was when we met all the Rollers in the VIP lounge of the airport. Just me, my mate and all five Rollers!

"Tina chatted to Eric, and I gave Ian a birthday present, and got his autograph.

"We found out something while we were in Scotland, and that is that if you go screaming after them, they won't take any notice of you, because they're scared.

"But if you walk up calmly to them, they'll stop and talk to you."

# THE BEST DAY OF MY LIFE....

**Michelle Edwards' hero isn't a pop star, but a footballer – gorgeous Kevin Keegan!**

"Kevin was recording a TV show at our local sports centre," she says, "and my mate Anne and I went down there in the hope that we'd catch a glimpse of him.

"It must have been our lucky day, cos when we went into the bar, the first person we saw was Kevin!

"We asked him for his autograph and he was really friendly to us. He even came outside so we could take some photos of him.

"I gave my camera to my mate and asked her to take a photo of Kevin and me – and he put his arm round me!"

## FAVOURITES!

"When we'd finished taking photos of him, Kevin chatted to Anne and me about our favourite team, Manchester United.

"Then he had to go out and do some filming for the show he was on, and Anne and I sat and watched the whole thing!

"Then at the end of the day, we were walking home when Kevin's car passed us.

"Luckily, there was a traffic jam, so the car stopped and Kevin asked us if we had our photos safe.

"We said we did, and then he had to move off, so Anne and I shouted, 'Bye Kevin!' and he said 'Bye loves!'

"And that was the end of our day with Kevin – one of the nicest people I've ever met!

"And definitely the nicest most unforgetable day of my life!"

# DONNY SMILED AT ME!

**Not too many groups visit New Zealand, where Mates reader Susan Davey lives. So when she heard the Osmonds were coming to her town, she decided that was too good an opportunity to miss!**

"As soon as I heard the Osmonds were coming to New Zealand, I booked seats for their concert," she says. "But that wasn't enough for me – I had to meet them as well!

"So a couple of days before they were due to arrive, my mate Janet and I made our plans!

"On the big day, we stayed off school and started phoning the local radio station to find out when they were arriving.

"In the end, they told us they'd already arrived and were on the way to their hotel. But no amount of begging would make them tell us the name of that hotel!

"By this time, my mum was getting as excited over the whole thing as we were, so she phoned up all the posh hotels in town asking if they were staying there!

"Finally, she found the right one and we jumped into the car and headed for the hotel!

"When we got there, we found four or five other fans there, so we sat in the lounge and waited for them to come down.

"After about fifteen minutes, one of the others shouted, 'It's Marie!' and we all dashed to meet her.

"Then Mary and Susanne came down, and told us they were going shopping.

"We were just recovering from seeing them when the lift doors opened, and out walked Mr. and Mrs. Osmond, Jimmy, Merrill, Alan and Jay!

"I was so busy talking to them that I didn't notice Donny arrive. Then I suddenly turned round . . . and there he was!

"Everyone was rushing to get his autograph, but he was ever so nice, and as he signed his name in my book, he gave me a huge smile . . . I still shake all over when I think of it!

"Next day at school, nobody believed us that we'd actually met the Osmonds. But we could prove it . . . cos we had a beautiful photo of us with Donny!"

# I COULDN'T BELIEVE THEY WERE REAL!

Jackie from Edinburgh says she's a mad Mud fan, so when she actually saw her faves in the flesh she could hardly believe they were real!

"I've seen Mud play live five times now," she says, "but at their last concert in Edinburgh, I decided I just had to meet 'em!

"Me an' my mates found out which hotel they were staying in, an' booked ourselves in for the night. (Phew – expensive but worth it!)

"When we saw their big blue Cadillac pull up outside the hotel, we ran down to meet them.

"My stomach was churning, and my hands were so clammy I could hardly hold my autograph book!

"The first person I saw getting out of the car was Dave Mount – an' I just burst into tears!

"He smiled and started chatting to me, an' soon we were all in the coffee lounge drinking coffee an' having a great laugh together.

"Les was sitting next to me, an' I just kept saying, 'Is it real?'

"We'd saved up for ages to buy each of the boys a tartan teddy bear, an' they were really pleased with 'em. They said they'd certainly remember Edinburgh now!

"We'd all brought cameras, an' we spent the rest of the afternoon getting autographs an' having photos taken.

"I was still in a daze!

"The concert that night was fantastic, an' afterwards, we sat up with the boys till nearly four in the morning, just talking! (Yawn . . .!)

"I'll never, ever forget that day, as long as I live!"

"At first you stayed faithful to her . . . It was easy until a friend asked you for help."

DO ME A FAVOUR, DAVE. THIS GIRL COUSIN IS STAYING WITH US FOR A COUPLE OF WEEKS AND I'M SUPPOSED TO LOOK AFTER HER. SHE'S A BIT DOWN, NEEDS COMPANY. IF YOU'D JUST MAKE UP A FOUR-SOME.

WELL, OKAY . . . BUT SHE COULD FIND I'M DULL COMPANY.

LOOK, I DON'T WANT TO SEEM RUDE, BUT . . . WELL, I'VE GOT A STEADY GIRL ONLY SHE'S AWAY . . . SO YOU SEE . . .

FOR ONCE THE MOUSE ISN'T GOING TO PLAY AROUND? OKAY, I WON'T BE INSULTED IF YOU DON'T MAKE A PASS AT ME.

SURE YOU WON'T BE TOO BORED?

I'LL SURVIVE.

HEY, FOLKS, COME ON — WE'RE GOING FOR A DRIVE!

MICK'S ALWAYS DOING CRAZY THINGS!

I KNOW, WE WERE AT SCHOOL TOGETHER. THEY USED TO CHAIN HIM UP DURING THE HOLIDAYS!

I MUST ADMIT IT'S A CHANGE FOR ME BEING HERE LIKE THIS, I MEAN. IN A PLACE LIKE THIS . . . NORMALLY, I'D BE . . .

WITH THE GIRL YOU LOVE — I KNOW WHAT YOU MEAN!

MIND YOU . . . HE SEEMS TO GET A LOT OF FUN OUT OF LIFE.

ROMANTIC SETTING, WARM EVENING . . . HE'S JUST DOING WHAT COMES NATURALLY!

"You did try keeping apart . . ."

I WON'T . . . I CAN'T CALL FOR HER . . !

"But it was no use."

DAVE, I – I HAD TO SEE YOU!

JOANNE – !

JOANNE, IF IT WASN'T FOR SARAH . . !

OH, DAVE . . !

DAVE, DON'T MAKE IT MORE DIFFICULT. I'VE COME TO SAY GOODBYE. I'M GOING HOME . . . I'LL WRITE, BUT THAT'S ALL.

I SEEM TO SPEND HALF MY LIFE HERE . . . SAYING GOODBYE TO SOMEONE!

BUT AT LEAST YOU'VE HAD THE COURAGE TO COME AND FIND THE FIRST GIRL AND TEST YOUR FEELINGS.

CAN YOU SEE WHAT SHE'S GOING TO SAY?

THE END

# STOP MOPING, CINDERS! GET UP AND HAVE A BALL!

So you've been going around lately with a face as long as a lampost, complaining that no fella would look twice at you if you were the last girl on earth . . . Well, no wonder!

Let's face it, mate, no fella's gonna look twice at you if you go around looking like the original heap of misery, now are they?

And who could blame 'em?

Bet you don't look at fellas who go around with their chins dragging on the ground. No, the ones you fancy are the ones who look like they've got a bit of life in them!

And the same goes for you. If you look like a drag, you're gonna be left to get on with it on your own.

So, snap out of it!

## FIND A FELLA

Okay, so you've got your mind right. You're going around looking bright and bouncy, with a permanent smile slapped across your chops, like the original Cheshire cat.

Well done! You're on your way . . .

(If in doubt, see pages 58 and 59 to find out how you can really get yourself feeling – and looking – great!)

Now, all you've got to do is grab yourself a guy. (This is the hard part, so pay attention!)

Unless you believe in miracles, of course, you can't expect him to come falling out of the sky. You've got to go out and get him! So, set working out a plan of action . . . The *where*, the *when* and the *how*.

## WHERE?

You may see dozens of tasty-looking fellas wandering around the streets that you'd just love to wrap up and take home. but it's not as easy as that!

Chances are, none of 'em are suddenly gonna stop dead in the middle of the High Street and ask you for a date – even if you do drop your hankie!

Nope, you've got to go some place where there's going to be a chance of getting into conversation with them.

The disco's an obvious place. More romances have started on the dance floor than anywhere.

And no wonder! There you are, done up like a dog's doodah, looking absolutely irresistible, with all that luscious music in the background, soft lights – in fact, the whole show! What could be more romantic than that?

So the disco's your number one bet. But it's not your only one.

Your youth club or sports club is a pretty good meeting place, too. You may feel a bit hot 'n' sweaty after a game of badminton, but just think of the roses it puts in your cheeks!

And, even if you just stand by and watch "him" play ping-pong, it's a perfect opportunity for starting up a conversation. So think up a few witty remarks to fling in his direction before you go along!

## WHEN?

The right time to meet a fella is when the right fella comes along!

But there are one or two rules you should remember . . .

Number one. Never try to chat him up when he's with his mates. Most fellas prefer to keep mates and girls separate. If you try to mix the two you could end up forcing him to treat you as a joke – just out of self-defence. He'll never forgive you if you start his mates tittering.

The same goes when he's with his folks. If you bump into him down the supermarket with his mum, keep it to a discreet smile or maybe a Hello. Anything more romantic than that will turn his cheeks as pink as a roll of Baby Blush loo paper!

And another thing, don't try to butt in if he's already with another girl! That'll only make you look like a grabber! Wait till he's on his own, then grab!

But, seriously, even if he has shown some interest in you, never try to stake your claim when there's another girl around – especially if she was there first!

Fellas hate scenes!

## HOW?

This is the tricky bit.

You've got him cornered and the moment is right . . . Now you don't dare put a foot wrong.

So play it by ear.

If he's a confident sort of fella, then try a few jokes. Put on the sexy, "femme fatale" act and really wow him.

If he's the quiet sort, start up a conversation about something that interests him. Could be sport, could be cars, could be pop.

You don't have to be an expert to make a few intelligent remarks, and once you get him going, he'll take over anyway.

Whatever you do, don't just stand there in silence . . . or your moment will be gone!

Once he's noticed you you're halfway there. Now all you've got to do is convince him that you're what he's been missing all his life! Keep him interested.

Whatever you do, once you've got your fella nabbed, never start taking him for granted. And don't let him take you for granted either!

Make sure your Prince Charming appreciates you – and have a ball! ★

100

# CHARMING!

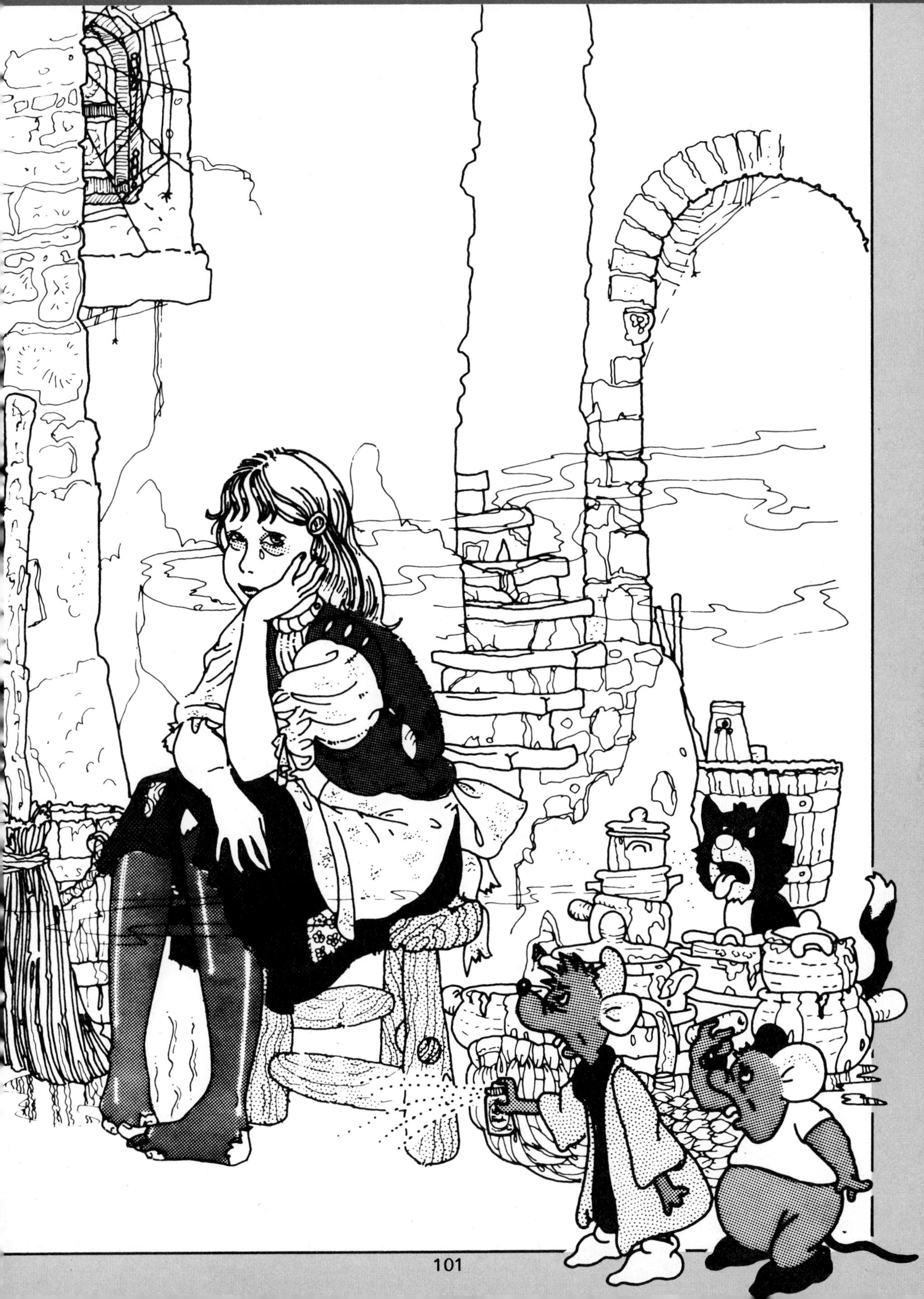

# ALAN'S HOUSE IS HAUNTED!

Since he left the Rollers, Alan Longmuir's lived by himself in a lonely farmhouse.

Well – not quite by himself. There's one other resident – a ghost!

"You can tell it's haunted," says brother Derek. "They say dogs can tell when there's ghosts around, an' it's true!

"As soon as they get near Alan's house, they start growling 'n' whimpering. An' if they're there at night, they keep getting up, going to the window and barking – as though they've heard someone outside!

"But that's not all. Alan's noticed lots of other strange things!

"F'rinstance, he goes out, 'n' switches all the lights off – but when he gets back, they're all on again!

"An' things get moved about – ornaments fall off the mantel piece, pictures come off the wall . . . all that sorta thing!

"But the weirdest thing was when Alan went to bed one night. It was really quiet – it is up there in the hills, so there's no traffic or anything.

"Alan was just settling down to sleep when he heard this weird sound out in the garden.

"He went an' looked out of the window, but he couldn't see anything, so he went back to bed.

"But as soon as he lay down, it started again—and this time he was sure it was coming from outside!

"An' this time round, he reailsed what the noise was. The sound of wood being chopped!

"After hearing that, I'd never stay at Alan's place overnight!

"He says it doesn't bother him, but cor . . . if I heard anything spooky, you wouldn't see me for dust!"  ★

# ROGER'S HAIR STOOD ON END!

Before he came to London and joined Queen, drummer Roger used to play with a local group in Cornwall.

"Did pretty well, too," he says. "We used to get regular bookings all over the county.

"Every Saturday night, f'rinstance, we played in this club. It was really spooky . . . built on the site of an ancient tin mine, an' supposed to be crawling with ghosts.

"I'd never really believed in ghosts up till then, but there was something strange about that place. You could sense the atmosphere.

"It wasn't too bad when there were lots of people around, but when the show was over, and we were left alone to pack up our gear, that's when it got to you!

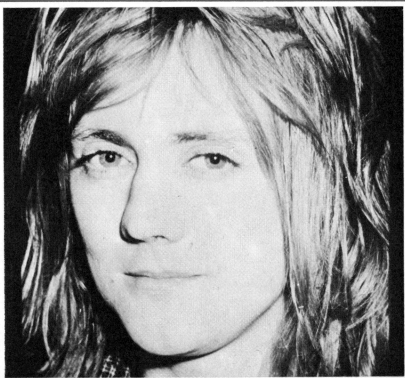

"One night, we'd packed up and were getting into our van when I realised I'd left my jacket in the dressing room!

"I went back inside, switched on the lights, and walked up the corridor. But as I got near to the dressing room, I heard someone moving about inside!

"I stopped to listen, and there it was again!

"Puzzled, I opened the door, stepped inside — and stopped dead!

"The room was pitch black and icy cold! As I stood there, a blast of cold air swept past, banging the door shut behind me!

"I swear my hair stood on end! I just stood there, too frightened to move, shivering all over — and I could hear footsteps walking away down the corridor!

"I must've stood there for about three minutes, without moving a muscle. Then as the footsteps died away, I ran!

"The others just laughed when I told 'em my story.

"But I don't care what they say. I did meet a ghost that night – I'm sure of that!" ★

# THE SPOOK TOOK BILLY BY SURPRISE!

**B**illy McIsaac of Slik didn't believe in ghosts . . . so when his mate told him his flat was haunted, he just laughed!

"He told me that every night, he could hear noises . . . chinks on the window, as though someone was chucking stones at it," he says.

"I didn't believe a word of it! So he dared me to stay at his place . . . said I'd hear it too!

" 'All right!' I said. 'You're on!'

"So we went back to his place about ten at night, and decided to wait up all night for the spook to turn up!

"We must've sat there till three, listening out for any noise. But as time wore on, nothing happened . . . and in the end, we fell asleep.

"When we woke up in the morning, I had a great laugh! 'See,' I said, 'it's all your imagination. There's no such thing as ghosts!'

"But he just shook his head. 'You'll see,' he said ominously. 'You'll see!'

'I didn't think any more of it till a couple of weeks later. We went to a late-night party, and I decided to stay at his place.

"But no sooner had I settled down to sleep than I was shocked awake! I could hear a noise on the window . . . a chinking sound, just like he'd described!

"I went over to the window, but there was nothing to be seen. But that didn't stop the noise! All night it went on — chink, chink, chink — always like that, in threes.

"Gradually, I stopped listening to it, and began to drift off. Then suddenly, I jumped a mile!

"There was a huge crash — and the mirror slid off the dressing table and smashed on the floor!

"By this time, my mate was awake too. 'See,' he whispered. 'That sort of thing happens all the time in this place. D'you believe me now?'

"I could only nod . . . I was speechless!

"I made sure I never stayed in that flat gain, but I kept in touch with that guy, and he told me strange things kept happening there.

"I don't know how he had the courage to stay on there. One night was enough for me, I can tell ya!" ★

# COR, WHY CAN'T

## ALL DOLLED UP!

The 'Dolls' in Guy'n'Dolls are really super lookers, aren't they?!

Even though they're on the go the whole time they always manage to look super cool. How do they do it?

Well, no chuckin' clothes on the floor or over chairs. When they've finished a show everything gets packed neatly away into their wardrobe ready for next time.

Sounds like a handy tip there, mates! You could try it, too!

## KEEP IT FUN, CHUM!

The Three Degrees always look a really cheeky bunch of girls! Noticed all their crazy accessories?!

For a real fun look go for thick shiny patent belts, or try a scarf tied peasant style round your head.

You're bound to catch a second glance from someone!

## NICE 'N' SIMPLE!

Kiki keeps it plain and simple but always manages to add a touch of sparkle somewhere. Like her patchwork belt, f'rinstance.

If you've got a plain dress that needs brightenin' up go for belts and badges or a shawl tied round your waist to add a bit of interest.

## ON THE GO WITH OLIVIA!

Here's Olivia Newton-John lookin' really relaxed after a jet set flight!

If you're travelling around like our Olivia keep clothes simple and to a minimum.

Jeans are great for this and with a roomy comfortable jacket too you should have an easy trip!

Well, you don't want to end up at your destination lookin' like a bunch of old rags, now do you?!

So if you keep to these superstar tips, who knows. You might even make number one in your fella's chart, eh?!

# LOOK LIKE HER?!

## STUNNIN' STOMPIN' SUZI!

If you're like Suzi and practically live in trousers, then get yourself some exciting tops to go with 'em!

Suzi's leather jacket looks really smart, but if you're not that flash with money then get some bright shirts'n'sweaters instead.

Tart 'em up with a scarf knotted round your neck! Looks great!

## SMART AS MARIE!

What with all her dishy brothers around no wonder Marie looks great and well groomed all the time!

Go for well-fitting clothes and nothing too fussy. Remember, you only look fatter in clothes that are too tight for you!

## RELAXIN' WITH LINDA!

With a bubbly personality like Linda's who's gonna notice what colour her tights are?!

Bet when you're sloppin' around at home it's in your Dad's old cardi eh?!

Why not get a kimono like Linda's. You can pick one up, buy one we mean, really cheaply in large department stores now.

Who knows when your fella's gonna turn up early for a date? So take a tip from Linda. You don't want to look like an old bag all the time, do you?!

## LOOKS LIKE LYNSEY!

Lynsey always looks just right whenever you see her. Makes you sick, doesn't it!

So even if you're only 5 foot tall like Lynsey you can still be noticed!

See all those super silver bits she's got all over herself?

Well, just don't stick to one ring or necklace, chuck the whole lot on for a really exciting look!

# mates

### SLIK

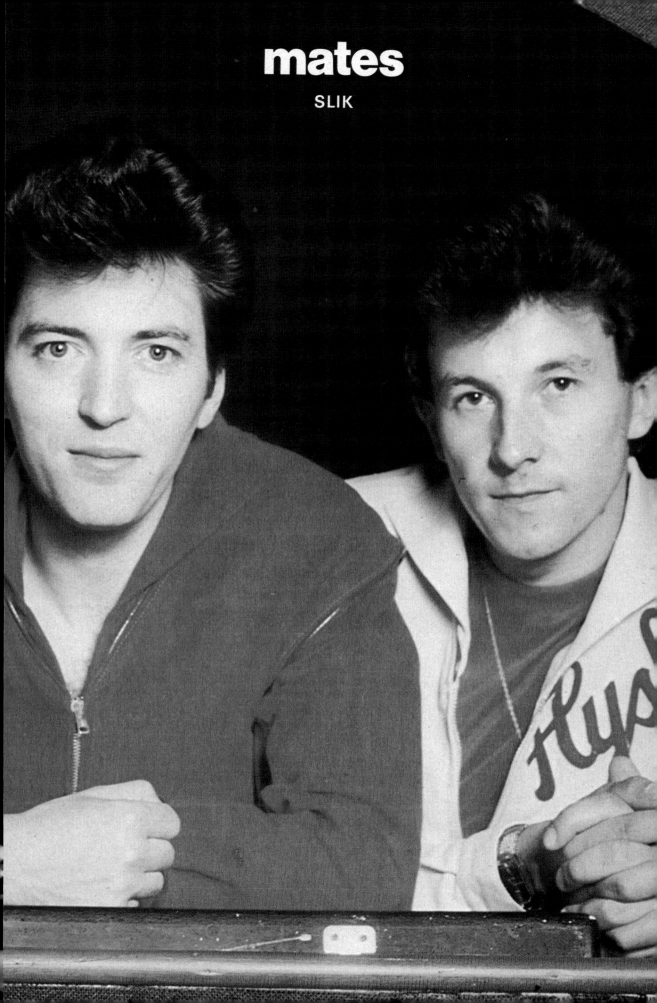

# mates

## SHOWADDYWADDY

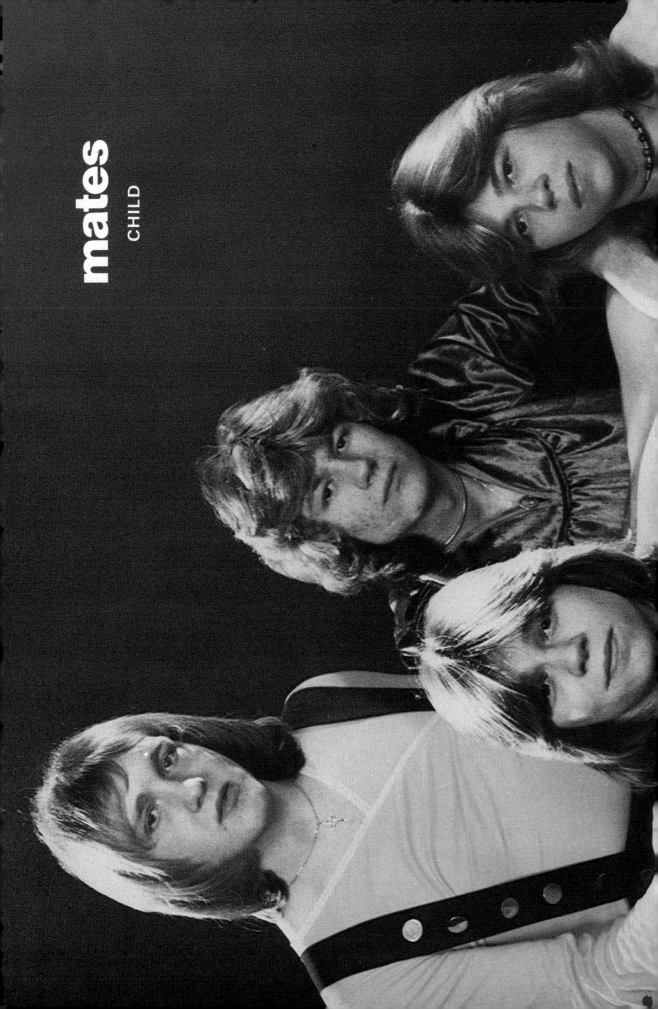

**mates**

CHILD

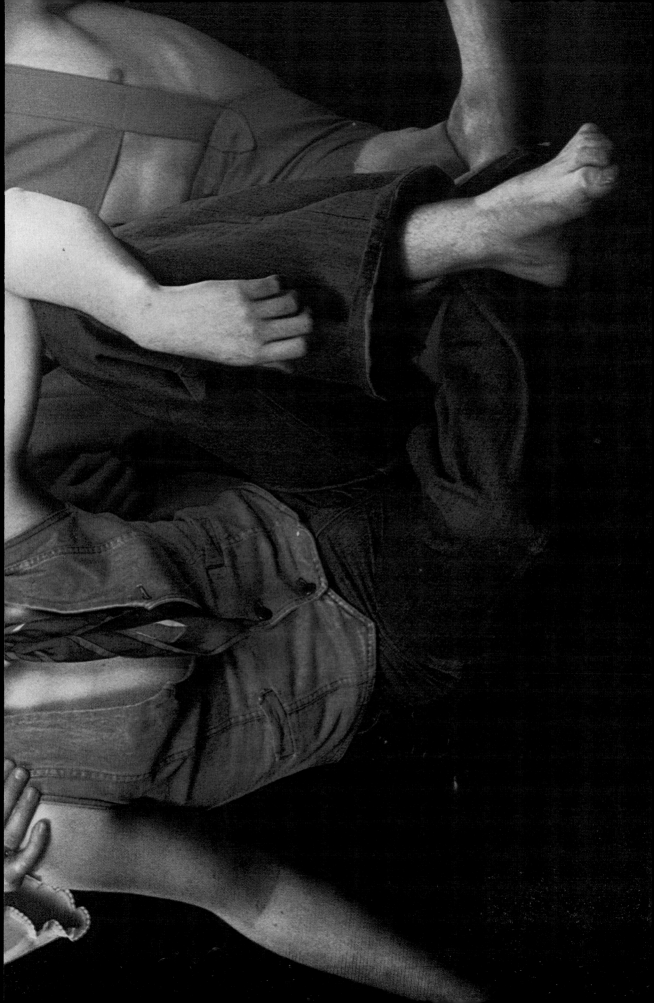

# WHAT'S

**Smelly feet, grotty spots, or just a touch of B.O.? Tell Suzi all your problems and she'll set you straight!**

**Dear Suzi,**
Whenever I pluck my eyebrows they end up bleeding and feeling really sore!

Sounds like a very painful job! It needn't be once you learn the knack!

First of all you want to decide what eyebrow shape you want.

Take a thin pencil and hold it upright against the side of your nose. Where it crosses your eyebrow is where the brow should start.

Now tip the pencil so that it makes a straight line from the edge of your nostril to the outer corner of your eye and beyond. This shows where your brow should end.

Hold the skin tight with one hand and with the other start plucking with a good pair of tweezers.

Never pluck eyebrows from the top of the brow 'cos this spoils the natural shape of the brow.

When you've finished rub a little antiseptic over the eyebrow so that the pores close up and don't turn into spots.

There that wasn't so painful, was it?!

**Dear Suzi,**
I've always had fat thighs and a huge bum.

**Even dieting never seems to work!**

Looks like you need some exercise, too!

Here's a good one for trimming off those extra fatty layers.

Sit upright on the floor with your back straight and legs stretched out in front of you.

Bend your right leg at the knee, leave the left one straight. Put your arms down beside you, hands flat on the floor. Raise yourself slightly and bounce really hard on your left cheek about 10 times.

Now stretch over and repeat on the right one about 2 times more.

Well if it doesn't work at least your bum should be a lovely black'n'blue colour!

**Dear Suzi,**
I've just started wearing make-up and haven't a clue about what brushes or applicators I'll need!

For a start you'll definitely need some cotton wool for taking off your make-up.

Get some baby cotton wool as this will be much cheaper than the surgical tye.

Then you'll certainly need a blusher brush for dusting on blusher or highlighter. They're also useful for brushing away any traces of eyeshadow that falls onto your cheeks.

Try baby cotton wool buds for putting on your eyeshadow with.

Next comes a lip brush which is really essential for a super outline to your lips. You could use a paint brush if you want to save a bit of money.

A wedge-shaped brush always comes in handy for applying shadow to the socket.

Now you should be fully equipped to put on a super face!

**Dear Suzi,**
No matter how often I wash my hair it's always greasy the next day!

It's probably your age that makes your hair as greasy as it is but I know that's never much help!

Get a good lemon shampoo that'll help right your greasy problem.

Eat lots of nourishing food and wash your brush'n' comb every week. Clean pillowcases help too.

Conditioning is O.K. as long as it's especially for oily hair.

# P NOW?!

It doesn't matter how often you wash your hair as long as you stick to a mild shampoo

**Dear Suzi,**
**As I wear specs I never know what sort of eye make-up to use!**

Just 'cos girls wear glasses it's never a waste of time to make-up your eyes. You'll be surprised what a difference it makes.

Use pretty colourful eye shadows 'cos the glasses cut out a lot of the light, so never use dark colours.

Put a shiny highlighter on your browbone, then a coloured shadow on the lid and around the underneath of the eye.

For mascara use a lash builder one. Apply several coats of this to your top and lower lashes.

If you've got tinted lenses use a deeper coloured shadow in the socket.

**Dear Suzi,**
**I've got such awful acne. I never want to go to the disco with my mates!**

Have you tried seeing a doctor? He ought to be able to recommend some cream or lotion for you to take.

Try these tips out yourself and you should notice a difference.

Avoid sweet and starchy foods like nuts, chocolate and fried food. Eat loads of fresh fruit and start each meal with half a grapefruit.

Everytime you wash use a medicated soap and use a clean flannel and towel as often as you can.

Get loads of fresh air and sun and you'll soon be on the way to a super clear skin!

**Dear Suzi,**
**All my mates pull my leg about my double chin. They all call me 'chubby chops' now!**

You'll need to do a few exercises to get yourself a slim chin!

Put some moisturiser onto your hands and stroke, with

the back of your hands up your throat and out under your chin. Go really fast for a few minutes.

Now lightly slap under your chin, still with the back of your hands, for a while.

You could camouflage it with some blusher. Brush it lightly under your chin to form a slight shadow.

**Dear Suzi,**
**I've got this awful birthmark on my cheek. It makes me very self conscious when I'm chatting to fellas.**

You can hide scars and birthmarks with a good stick make-up.

Pat on your normal foundation, then using the stick make-up dab a little onto the mark.

Blend this into your foundation. Dust lightly with a little powder to set the make-up. If you're really worried about it go and see your doctor.

**Dear Suzi,**
**I've got these horrid, small piggy eyes. What's the best make-up to use to get 'em looking bigger?**

Get your eyebrows plucked first to give yourself a larger eye area to play around with.

Put a shiny highlighter in white on your browbone and eyelid.

Use a dark shadow in the socket and underneath the eye. You could use a kohl pencil and make a line on the lower lid to give a more positive shape to your eye.

Now mascara the top and bottom lashes.

**Dear Suzi,**
**I always end up with wet patches under my arms. I can't help it but I just can't stop sweating when it starts heating up!**

Don't worry, we've all got to sweat sometime, but some more than others!

What's really nasty is the smell that goes with it!

Keep your underarms free from hair and wash twice a day. Use a good deodorant or anti-perspirant.

Whichever product you prefer put it on in the morning and also during the day immediately after washing.

If you can't have a bath every day then thoroughly wash yourself at the sink.

Another useful tip is to wear natural fabrics like cotton and wool, nylon stops the skin from breathing and causes sweatiness.

# STARS OF THE SMALL SCREEN!

Now that Richard O'Sullivan, better known to viewers as the accident prone Robin Tripp, has started his own bistro in the "Robin's Nest" series let's hope he doesn't get into as many scrapes!

In real life Richard is a true professional and started acting in films before he could even talk!

In his spare time he's an avid football freak, and plays golf as well.

His main interest is composing and playing music on the piano!

## COOLSOME TWOSOME!

*Seems like only yesterday that Paul Michael Glaser and David Soul first appeared on our screens as the fearless cops "Starsky and Hutch" – but they've been around two years!*

*Paul (Starsky) was born on March 25, 1943 in Cambridge, Massachusetts. He went to Tulane University and gained a degree in theatre. Then took a degree at Boston University in acting and directing. Clever lad! Paul lives in Hollywood and keeps in shape playing tennis.*

*David Soul's (Hutch) real surname is Solberg and his father is a Professor of Religion!*

*Besides acting, David's other mad passion is music! In fact, he was a successful singer in the days before "Starsky and Hutch" brought him fame on the telly screen.*

*Let's hope 1978 will bring us even more of this gorgeous twosome!*

*We'll be keeping a sharp lookout, that's for sure!*

## CHEEKY CHEF!

That cheeky, lopsided grin could only belong to the telly's favourite "chef"!

## MICK OF MAGPIE

Mick Robertson was born on St. Valentine's Day (when else!) in Petworth, West Sussex.

He went to Midhurst Grammar School and then on to Goldsmith's College, London to take a teaching diploma in drama.

Mick's 6' 1'' tall, has blue/grey eyes and luscious brown curly hair you'd just love to run your fingers through!

He claims his favourite

indoor sport is sleeping! Lazy thing!

Still, here's hoping he manages to stay awake long enough to keep making those telly appearances of his!

## BEN MURPHY

*Wasn't it great seeing actor Ben Murphy back on the screens again in "Gemini"! None of us have really got over him from the days of "Alias Smith and Jones"!*

## GET "SWEENEY"!

That cheeky face hasn't changed much from the days Dennis was an eleven-year-old-star in his own series "Just William"!

Ben's 5' 11" tall, doesn't smoke or drink and exercises daily to keep his steady weight.

He's single and loves blind dates! It's no wonder Ben was once labelled the "World's Greatest Lover!" Can't be bad!

Dennis was born on February. 28, 1948, which makes him a Pisces!

His favourite food is Sunday roasts and he drinks anything!

Besides acting, Dennis is also pursuing a recording career.

## OH, MOTHER!

Cor, wouldn't you just love to mother Michael Crawford, star of "Some Mothers Do 'Ave 'Em!" He's gorgeous!

Michael's a Capricorn — born on January 19 in Salisbury. He's 5' 10½" tall and weighs 9¾ stone and he says it's "all muscle"!

His favourite food is stews and his favourite football team is Queens Park Rangers. He tries to get along to their matches whenever possible.

He likes punctuality and a sense of humour and dislikes lateness, rudeness and selfishness.

That's fair enough!

# ALWAYS SECOND BEST!

With a mate as gorgeous as Ginny was, how could I ever expect any fella to fall for mousey little me? Especially any fella as fanciable as this one!

never had to imagine very hard what it's like to have a best mate who outshines in just about everything . . . Yeah, you name it, Ginny had t – and did it – ten times better than I ever could!

Trouble was, despite all the hardships of being the best buddy of someone as sexy, vivacious, likeable and cunning as Ginny – despite all the fellas I found (hopefully), lost (bitterly) and found again (sympathetically) when she'd finished with 'em – despite all this, I liked . . . nay loved! the girl dearly!

Oh, I knew she was no good for me . . . The strain was too much for my ego – after two years of "going on the razzle" (as she called it) with Ginny, my poor bruised, battered ego was so deflated I sometimes wondered if it was there at all.

But when we teamed up in the first year, how was I to know my lanky pal would emerge as the blonde, long-legged bombshell she is today?

I was the one all the fellas chatted to to get to Ginny . . . the sly, tactical approach, it was. It took me a while to cotton on, too.

I don't exactly look like the back of a bus, but I was always pleasantly surprised when some fantastic-looking fella started chatting *me* up. I could hardly believe my luck . . . Me? Sure you wanta to talk to me? I'd say to myself.

To begin with, I really believed they were interested in me, too . . . Then I got to know the signs. I'd usually count to anything up to

sentence ten – then the questions about Ginny would poke up their weary little heads . . .

"Good dancer, you friend, isn't she?" they'd say, their eyes riveted to the spot where Ginny was bopping in her split-to-the-thigh skirt. Or, a little more subtle . . . "I'm sure I've seen your friend somewhere before. What's her name?"

## CHEEKY!

Once I even had a "And how about introducing us, there's a doll!" Cheeky blighter! Believe me, it pained me tell some gorgeous hunk (and the ones who set their sights on Ginny usually were) to "go and get stuffed". But, well, I didn't like being Ginny's side-kick very much – however much I liked her.

"Ruthie – what's the matter?" she'd say, returning from a whirl with some fella on the dance floor, with usually three others buzzing around. "You look upset."

"Oh, nothing . . . That boy, er, just trod on my foot," I'd fib. How could I tell her I felt angry, upset and plain jealous all rolled into one . . .

And it was even worse when she'd inevitably end with the very fella I'd sent packing and had to thank *him* for giving me a lift home!

Well, as I say, I was no competition for Ginny's movie star looks, but eventually I did discover that small girls with long black hair, pale faces and eyes like saucers *can* be to some fellas' liking.

Make-up I tried. Made to-tease

clothes I tried. But it all went out the window – it just wasn't my style. "They", I decided, could either take me as I was or they wouldn't take me at all. Which, I'm sad to say, was always the case.

I tried not to be jealous of Ginny but when she managed to sweep people everywhere (okay, then – *boys* everywhere!) off their feet whereas I left 'em plain frozen to the spot, I began to feel that everything was down to stunning looks and charm-the-hind legs-off-a-donkey conversation.

It's all right being shy and stunning, or vivacious and not-so-stunning – but I was not-so-stunning and shy with it. I just couldn't win. So changes a-had to come . . .

But not quite the way I was expecting!

## RIDICULOUS

Off we were to the usual weekend haunt – the Greengage Disco. Tonight was slightly different – it was my birthday. So did at least feel that it was "my" night for a change.

I even sported the new stretchy tube top Ginny had bought me – very daring for me, it was, baring a bit of shoulder. I plastered on a bit of the ol' warpaint, too (make-up to you!) but somehow as soon as Ginny's more-glam-than usual apparation appeared through the door, I realised how ridiculous I looked.

The whole thing – it just wasn't *me*. After a silent bit of soul-searching and I-don't really-care-if-Ginny's-the-one-all-the-fellas-fall-for reasoning, I decided that someone, someday, would have to love me just the way I was – dark, pale-faced and saucer-eyed . . .

So, the whole lot came off (much to Ginny's sighings and "Oh, you looked so nice, Ruthie"), make-up, tube-top – the lot.

And on went my faithful old

CONTINUED ON PAGE 118

CONTINUED FROM PAGE 117

jeans (well, they were a good fit) and khaki shirt (a bargain for 5p at a local jumble). Then, without further ado on my part we set off, Ginny in her satin thigh-high dress with the fringes, making us look a bit like a "before and after of how to look trendy"!

"If a fella so much as whispers a question about you tonight I shall chuck my fizz-pop in his face!" I said, as we paid to go in.

"Oh, Ruth, you're exaggerating!" squeaked Ginny in her high, breathless voice. "You know how fellas try to make conversation about stupid things . . ."

"Yeah, twenty Ginny question, I reckoned! Anyway, is Sam coming tonight?"

Sam, for your information, was the latest, faithful Ginny victim.

"'Course!" she said, a bit matter-of-factly. "I said I'd see him here."

"Oh-ho — on the way out then, is he?" I always knew the signs . . .

"No," said Ginny, sheepishly. "It's just that — well, it's your birthday, isn't it?"

Yeah, she'd probably already got her eye on some lucky, unsuspecting fella. Ginny always looked at least one fella ahead . . .

## KISS GOODNIGHT

I must admit, as evenings go, I had a real fun time. There were some of my other school mates there, so we all joined up in a group. Lots of giggling and jiving around! I collapsed alongside Ginny for a breather, exhausted and happy.

Sometimes, it was nice not having the complication of a fella around, I decided . . . Not that my record to date of nil boyfriends (well, you can't really count three unsuccessful blind dates, can you?) to Ginny's eleven and a half (the half was poor old Sam, who currently didn't look as tho' he'd be amounting to much more than that) was anything to boast about.

To put it mildly, my experience was non-existent. Fifteen and I'd never even had a proper kiss goodnight! Well, I only knew that when Mr. Right did come along, he'd well 'n' truly knock me off me feet!

Now Ginny was alone. Apparently, Sam'd turned up and soon went off drinking with his mates at the bar. He seemed to be letting Ginny cool off — they'd had a blasting row as soon as he'd got there. Yup, now I definitely knew he was due to be ditched. Maybe things could be patched up, but, well, my birthday evening'd only just begun, so I certainly didn't fancy playing matchmaker tonight.

Anyway, something cunning was cookin' in that pretty little blonde head of Gin's.

She was sitting there looking very down-in-the mouth — that pursed-lip "Doesn't anyone want me?" hurt look.

"C'mon — out with it!" I said. "Who is it, this time?"

She sighed. "Well, if you must know, it's him." And she flashed a glance across the dance floor.

"Who?"

"Him, silly. Can't you see — he's absolutely gorgeous." Sigh.

Well, I must admit — it wasn't difficult to pick "him" out — tall, curly dark hair, baggy dungarees — he was just her style. And the

more I looked, the more I began to think he was my style, too!

"He was here last weekend . . . and kept smiling at me all the time over Sam's shoulder . . . I wish he'd do something about it!"

Well, I'd been grown-up sitting for Gran last week-end — and anyway, I wouldn't have forgotten him in a hurry. Just my luck, wasn't it, that Ginny was after him. What chance would I stand?

## GOOD LOOKING

I couldn't help saying it — when it seemed to me Ginny was sitting there with so much — while I had nought at all.

"Anyway, what's so wrong about Sam?" Poor fella, he was crazy about her.

"Oh, Ruth — you'll understand one day. Always ditch a boy before he ditches you. It only makes sense. Anyway, Sam's getting too possessive . . ."

And there was the poor fella watching every move she made.

"Do me a favour, Ruthie. When he comes over, well, would you keep Sam sort of occupied. Mm?"

I sat there, just for a second, thinking "Some birthday", when I noticed Ginny's eyes light up.

You guessed it, as usual, Ginny's charms had worked, like a dream. Suddenly, it was him looming over us . . .

Close-up, he wasn't what you'd call classically good-looking, he just had this incredible kinda crooked smile. Just for a crazy moment, I thought it might've been for me . . .

"Well, I'd better scram," I thought, suddenly finding it very hard to lift my feet. I made a move to pass him, then there was a firm grip on my arm — his!

"Hey — where're you off to? Surely the most lovely girl in the entire discotheque isn't going to refuse me a dance?"

"I — er me?"

He glanced down at me with piercing blue eyes and laughed.

"Yes — you!" and hugged me to him, then and there, right in front of Ginny.

Funny, in just one second, I suddenly felt the most beautiful, wanted and special girl in the world.

I smiled back at him, I couldn't help it — for once, I wasn't giving Ginny a thought . . . ★

Talk about eye-catching! This little lot have certainly got what it takes to make an impact on their audience! And their music's not bad either . . .

## ELTON SPECTACULAR!

Elton's famous for his spectacular specs, but this lot's really run riot. He looks like a cross

## MERCURY MARVEL!

Is it a bird? Is it a plane? No, it's just Freddie Mercury of Queen takin' off with gusto at one of their concerts a couple of years back!

Wouldn't fancy ironing that lot, would you?

## OH, LA LA!

Rock group Labelle must be one of the most extravagant trio of ladies around — remember their "Lady Marmalade" smash-hit of a couple of years back?

Reckon they make the Three Degrees look like a bunch of nuns!

between a bird of paradise and a fireworks display!

What we wonder is how does he manage to find the keyboard underneath all that lot!

Keep it up, Elton!

## DAVID'S WAY OUT!

Well, half out, anyway! Just hope that left arm doesn't get frostbite!

Before David Bowie took to the cropped hair and baggy suits look, he was famous for his spectacular stage gear. Folk used to go along to his concerts just to see what he looked like!

# GET A LOAD O' THEM!

123

THE END

# 'WE'RE HERE TO HELP YOU...'

Every week in Mates we're there to help you. Suzi for beauty, Carly for fashion and Maggie if you're just feeling blue.

Write to us any time and we'll see what we can do.

---

Dear Maggie,

I've been going out with this fella for about six weeks and I really think that I love him.

The trouble is, that although he says he loves me he keeps putting off our dates to go out with his mates. He's done this three times in the past two weeks, and it really upsets me a lot.

My mate says I'm silly to put up with him and that I should chuck him, but I love him too much to do that.

What can I do?

Well, for a start, you've got to make up your mind yourself and not go listening to what your mate says! Could be she's just jealous!

And then you've got to sort out with this fella of yours exactly what is going on. Fair enough if he wants to go out with his mates sometimes, but he shouldn't have to break dates with you to do it!

Tell him you don't mind him going

out with his mates, but he's got to stop mucking you around. Maybe you could agree to keep certain days of the week specially for seeing friends — and then you can fix up to go out with your friends, too.

Then you can fix up to see each other on the other days and he'll have no excuse for letting you down.

If he continues to break dates, though, you should start wondering seriously if he's really worth all the heartache.

Could be he's just not emotionally ready yet to go out with a girl on a regular basis, and is really happier with his friends. In that case, the best thing you can do, for both your sakes, is just leave him to it!

Dear Maggie,

Just recently my best mate's started going out with a boy and it seems to have become very serious. Before she met him we used to always go out together in a crowd, but now there's always just the two of them on their own.

I wouldn't mind, but for some reason she's started making fun of me because I don't have a steady boyfriend of my own. Every time I meet her she keeps making nasty jokes about it.

If it wasn't for this I would be quite happy to continue going out in a crowd, but now I'm beginning

---

# DOCTOR'S ORDERS!

Dear Doctor,

Every time I have a period the pain's so bad that I have to take pain-killers, especially the first few days.

My mum says that it'll get better as I get older, but one of my mates told me that this isn't true.

Does this mean I'll have pain every month for the rest of my life?

I hope not. Usually, as your mum told you, period pain gets less as you get older, but unfortunately it doesn't always go away altogether.

If the pains are very bad, go along to your doctor and ask him to prescribe something specially for period pains.

Dear Doctor,

My front teeth are in good condition, but they're not very white.

I've been thinking I might get them capped. What do you think?

I think it would be a shame to have perfectly sound teeth capped just for cosmetic reasons — unless, of course, they are very badly discoloured.

Ask your dentist. He should know if it's worth going ahead.